Marketing & Business Essentials

CHERI MITCHELL

JEROME LAWRENCE

ISBN: 9798344676111

DEDICATION

To family and friends, People First of Lithonia Stonecrest, and to my husband the best artist ever Jerome Lawrence.

Contents

ACKNOWLEDGMENTS

Thanks for the help of Jerome Lawrence with computer and document formatting expertise. I am also grateful for the help of members of People First of Stonecrest remembering our many discussions on marketing and business operations.

Part 1: Introduction to Marketing and Business Operations

Chapter 1: The Role of Marketing in Business

Marketing plays a key role in the success of any business, whether large or small. But what exactly is marketing, and why is it so important? In simple terms, marketing is about getting your product or service noticed by the right people, at the right time, and at the right price. It's like telling the story of your business in a way that makes people want to buy from you.

Think of marketing as the bridge between a business and its customers. It helps you connect with the people who need or want what you're offering, guiding them through the process of discovering, evaluating, and ultimately purchasing your product or service.

The Purpose of Marketing

At its core, marketing is all about sales. The ultimate goal is to get more people to buy your product or service. But it's not just about making sales today; it's about creating relationships with customers that will keep them coming back in the future. Good marketing makes your business stand out, builds trust with your audience, and convinces people that what you're offering is worth their time and money.

Marketing also helps businesses understand their audience better. Through research and feedback, you learn what your customers like, what they don't like, and what problems they need solving. This information is incredibly valuable because it allows you to adjust your marketing strategies to better meet customer needs, which leads to more sales in the long run.

The Importance of Continuous Marketing

Marketing isn't something you do once and then forget about. It's an ongoing process that evolves as your business grows and as the market changes. Think about it like planting a garden—you don't just plant the seeds and walk away. You water them, give them sunlight, and make sure the soil is healthy so the plants can grow. Similarly, marketing needs constant attention to make sure your business continues to thrive.

Regular marketing efforts help keep your brand in the minds of customers. If they don't hear from you, they might forget about you or turn to your competitors. By staying active with marketing, you remind customers of the value you provide and why they should choose your product or service over others.

How to Approach Marketing

Approaching marketing is like putting together a puzzle. There are many different pieces—like advertising, pricing, and customer engagement—that need to fit together to create a complete picture. One of the most important pieces is your **elevator pitch**. An elevator pitch is a brief, clear explanation of what your business does and why people should care about it. Imagine you're in an elevator with someone, and you only have the time it takes to reach your floor to explain your business. What would you say to grab their attention?

For example, if you own a bakery, your elevator pitch might be: "We bake fresh, homemade cookies every morning using organic ingredients and unique family recipes. Our customers love the rich flavors and knowing they're getting something made with love."

A good elevator pitch makes people curious about your business and interested in learning more. It should be short, simple, and focused on what makes your product or service special.

The Four P's of Marketing

To build a successful marketing strategy, you need to think about what marketers call "The Four P's." These are the key areas you need to focus on to make sure your marketing efforts are effective:

1. **Product**: What are you selling? You need to clearly understand your product or service and what makes it different from others on the market. This will help you identify the right audience and figure out how to talk about your product in a way that resonates with them.
2. **Price**: How much will you charge for your product? Pricing is tricky because you need to find the right balance between what customers are willing to pay and what it costs you to make the product. You also have to think about how your pricing compares to your competitors.
3. **Place**: Where will you sell your product? This could be in a physical store, online, or through a third-party retailer. You need to choose the places where your customers are most likely to find and buy your product.
4. **Promotion**: How will you get the word out about your product? Promotion includes advertising, public relations, sales promotions, and any other way you can think of to generate interest and excitement about your product.
5. By focusing on these four areas, you can create a marketing plan that reaches the right people and encourages them to buy your product.

Marketing is a vital part of any business because it helps you connect with your customers, build relationships, and drive sales. It's not something you can do once and forget about—it's an ongoing process that requires constant attention and adjustment. By understanding your product, pricing it correctly, choosing the right places to sell it, and promoting it effectively, you'll set your business up for success. Keep working on your elevator pitch and think about how to incorporate the Four P's into your strategy, and you'll be well on your way to becoming a marketing pro!

Chapter 2: Ongoing Marketing Strategies

Marketing doesn't stop after you make your first sale or launch your first advertisement. In fact, successful businesses are always marketing. But why? Because the marketplace is always changing—new products are coming out, new competitors are entering the scene, and customers' needs and preferences are constantly evolving. So, to stay relevant and keep attracting customers, you need ongoing marketing strategies.
Let's break down why continuous marketing is important and how to keep it going in a way that helps your business grow.

Why Continuous Marketing Matters

Imagine you're running a lemonade stand. The first day, you make a lot of sales because people are excited about trying something new. But if you don't keep telling people about your lemonade, they might forget you're there or choose to buy from a new lemonade stand down the street. This is where continuous marketing comes in—it keeps reminding people about your product and why they should choose you over your competitors.
Here are a few reasons why ongoing marketing is crucial:

1. **Keeping Your Brand in the Spotlight**: If people don't hear about your business regularly, they might forget about you. Regular marketing efforts keep your brand fresh in their minds.
2. **Building Stronger Relationships with Customers**: Marketing helps you stay connected with your customers. Through emails, social media, or special offers, you can remind them why they love your product and keep them coming back.
3. **Adapting to Changes**: The market is always changing, and your customers' needs might shift over time. By regularly evaluating and updating your marketing strategies, you can adapt to these changes and make sure you're still offering something valuable.
4. **Staying Ahead of Competitors**: In a competitive world, you need to stay one step ahead. Continuous marketing helps you maintain your edge, making sure you're the go-to choice for customers even as new competitors emerge.

How to Keep Your Marketing Strategy Fresh

Now that we know why ongoing marketing is important, let's talk about how you can keep your marketing strategy fresh and effective. Here are some ways to make sure your marketing is always working for you:

1. **Constantly Evaluate Your Strategy**
   It's important to take a step back every now and then and ask, "Is this working?" Maybe a particular social media post got a lot of attention, or maybe a sale didn't go as well as you hoped. Take note of what's working and what's not. From there, you can tweak your approach to make sure you're always improving.
2. For example, if you're running an Instagram account for your business, check which posts get the most likes and comments. Are they videos? Photos of your products? Quotes? Once you know what your audience likes, you can create more content that resonates with them.
3. **Keep Your Elevator Pitch Ready**
   An elevator pitch is a quick, catchy way to explain your business. Even though it's something simple, it needs to evolve as your business grows. What worked as your pitch when you started might not be the best reflection of where your business is now.
4. Let's say you started a business selling handmade bracelets, but now you've expanded into selling rings and necklaces too. Your elevator pitch might need to change from "I sell handmade bracelets" to "I create handmade, custom jewelry that adds a unique touch to any outfit."
5. **Update Your Marketing Channels**
   Your customers might not be in the same place they were a year ago. Maybe they've switched from Facebook to TikTok, or maybe they've started using a new app for shopping. It's important to keep track of where your customers are spending their time and make sure your marketing is reaching them there.
6. Don't be afraid to explore new marketing channels, like trying out a podcast, starting a YouTube channel, or experimenting with influencer marketing.

Balancing Online and Offline Marketing

Marketing has changed a lot in the past decade, with the rise of digital marketing. While online marketing is important, it doesn't mean you should completely forget about offline marketing strategies. The best approach is often a balance of both.

1. **Online Marketing**:
   This is where most businesses focus nowadays because people spend a lot of time online. Online marketing includes things like social media ads, email marketing, blog posts, and SEO (search engine optimization). This type of marketing lets you reach a wide audience, often with lower costs than traditional marketing.
   - **Social Media**: Platforms like Instagram, TikTok, and Twitter are great for connecting with your audience in real-time.
   - **Email Marketing**: Regularly sending emails with updates, discounts, or helpful tips keeps customers engaged.
   - **SEO**: Making sure your website appears in search results when people look for products like yours.
2. **Offline Marketing**:
   Though online marketing is popular, traditional marketing still works, especially in local areas. Offline marketing includes things like flyers, billboards, and in-store promotions. It's a great way to reach people who might not be on social media or who respond better to physical advertisements.
   - **Billboards and Posters**: Eye-catching designs can still grab people's attention in public spaces.
   - **Event Marketing**: Hosting or sponsoring local events can help get the word out about your business and build personal connections with potential customers.
3. The key is to figure out which mix works best for your business and your audience.

Tracking Your Marketing Efforts

Once you've got your ongoing marketing strategy in place, it's important to keep track of how it's performing. This way, you know what's working and what might need to change.

- **Set Clear Goals**:
  Do you want to get more followers on social media? Increase your sales by a certain percentage? Whatever your goals are, write them down so you can measure your success.
- **Use Analytics Tools**:
  There are many tools available to help you track your marketing efforts. For example, Google Analytics can show you how many people visit your website, and social media platforms offer insights into how well your posts are performing.
- **Adjust as Needed**:
  If something isn't working as well as you'd hoped, don't be afraid to make changes. Marketing is all about experimenting and learning from what works best.

Ongoing marketing is like maintaining a good friendship—you have to keep checking in, offering value, and staying connected. It's about constantly evaluating your strategy, updating your approach, and making sure your message is reaching the right people. By doing this, you'll not only keep your current customers engaged, but you'll also attract new ones along the way. Remember, marketing is an ongoing journey, not a one-time event. Keep experimenting, keep learning, and most importantly, keep connecting with your customers.

Chapter 3: Crafting an Effective Elevator Pitch

Imagine you're in an elevator with someone who could help your business, but you only have the time it takes to reach the top floor to explain what your business is all about. What do you say? How do you make it sound exciting, clear, and memorable? This is where your elevator pitch comes in.
An **elevator pitch** is a short, persuasive speech that you can use to explain your business or idea in the time it takes to ride an elevator—usually about 30 seconds to a minute. It's like giving someone a teaser or trailer of your business, just like a movie trailer that gets you hooked without giving away the entire story.

Why is an Elevator Pitch Important?

You never know when you might meet someone important—whether it's a potential customer, a business partner, or even an investor. Being prepared with a strong, clear pitch can make all the difference in leaving a good impression. An elevator pitch helps you:

1. **Grab Attention Quickly**: In today's fast-paced world, people don't have time to listen to long explanations. Your pitch needs to grab their attention right away, just like how the opening lines of a great movie get you interested from the start. Think of it like the famous quote from *The Godfather*: "I'm gonna make him an offer he can't refuse." A good elevator pitch should be just as compelling.
2. **Make People Remember You**: A well-delivered pitch can stick in someone's mind, making them think about your business even after the conversation ends. Just like how a catchy song stays with you long after it's played, you want your pitch to be memorable.
3. **Open Doors for Future Opportunities**: Even if someone isn't ready to buy from you or invest in your idea right now, your pitch might spark enough interest for them to reach out in the future.

How to Create a Great Elevator Pitch

So, how do you craft an elevator pitch that works? It's easier than you might think if you break it down into simple steps:

1. **Start with Your Name and Business**
Introduce yourself right away. People need to know who you are and what you represent. This part is straightforward: "Hi, I'm Alex, and I run a business that sells eco-friendly clothing."
2. **Identify the Problem You Solve**
Next, explain what problem your business solves. This is where you show why your product or service matters. For example: "A lot of people want to buy clothes that are better for the environment, but they don't know where to find them. My business provides fashionable, sustainable clothing options."
3. **Highlight the Benefits**
Why should someone care about your solution? This is where you quickly list the benefits or unique features of your business. You might say: "Our clothes are made from recycled materials, and we plant a tree for every purchase, helping customers feel good about their choices while looking great."
4. **Call to Action**
Wrap up with what you want the listener to do next. Whether it's checking out your website, scheduling a meeting, or following you on social media, give them something simple to do after hearing your pitch. For example: "If you're interested in learning more, check out our website or visit our Instagram page for new collections."
5. **Keep It Simple and Clear**
Remember, you only have about 30 seconds. The key is to keep your message clear and not overload it with too many details. As the saying goes, "Keep it simple, stupid" (KISS method). Your pitch should be like a well-edited tweet—short, sweet, and to the point.

Example of a Strong Elevator Pitch

Let's imagine you run a local bakery that specializes in unique, custom cakes. Here's how your elevator pitch might sound:
"Hi, I'm Jamie, and I own Sweet Creations, a bakery that makes custom cakes for special events. We create cakes that don't just look good—they taste amazing, too! Whether it's a birthday, wedding, or any celebration, we design cakes based on your personal style. You can check out our latest designs on Instagram, and we'd love to make your next event sweeter!"
In this example:

- Jamie introduces themselves and the business right away.

- They explain what makes their business special (custom cakes that are delicious and designed based on personal style).
- They invite the listener to check out their Instagram to learn more.

Elevator Pitch Tips

- **Practice Makes Perfect**: Just like with anything else, practice helps you get better. Say your elevator pitch out loud several times until it feels natural. You want to sound confident and conversational, not like you're reading off a script.
- **Tailor Your Pitch to Your Audience**: If you're talking to an investor, you might focus on the financial potential of your business. If you're speaking with a potential customer, focus more on how your product will benefit them.
- **Stay Enthusiastic**: People are more likely to be excited about your business if you're excited about it! Your enthusiasm can make a big difference in how your pitch is received.

The KISS Method for Elevator Pitches

A famous technique for keeping things simple is the **KISS Method**, which stands for **Keep It Simple, Stupid**. This doesn't mean you're calling anyone "stupid." Instead, it's a reminder to avoid overcomplicating things. Simplicity is powerful. The easier it is for people to understand what you do, the more likely they are to remember it.

Even Steve Jobs, the co-founder of Apple, understood the importance of simplicity. He once said, "Simple can be harder than complex: You have to work hard to get your thinking clean to make it simple." Your elevator pitch should follow this idea—clean, simple, and effective.

Using Your Elevator Pitch in Different Situations

Your elevator pitch isn't just for business meetings. You can use it in many situations, such as:

- **Networking Events**: When you meet new people in your industry.
- **Job Interviews**: To explain your personal strengths and goals.
- **Social Media**: When introducing your business in a short video or post.
- **School Projects**: If you're presenting an idea or project to a group.

Crafting a great elevator pitch is like telling a short story about your business that gets people interested and wanting to learn more. By focusing on what problem you solve, what makes your business unique, and giving people a simple action to take, you can create a pitch that works in any situation. Just remember to keep it simple, stay confident, and practice until it feels natural. And as the great Albert Einstein once said, "If you can't explain it simply, you don't understand it well enough." So, work on making your pitch as clear and simple as possible—because that's when it really starts to work!

Chapter 4: The Four P's of Marketing

When you think about marketing, it might seem complicated with so many things to consider. But to make it easier, marketing can be broken down into four key parts, known as **The Four P's**: **Product**, **Price**, **Place**, and **Promotion**. These are the building blocks of any marketing strategy. Think of them like ingredients in a recipe: if you use the right amounts of each, you'll end up with a successful dish—your business.

Let's break down each of these "P's" so you can understand how to use them in your marketing strategy.

---

1. Product: What Are You Selling?

The first "P" stands for **Product**. This is the thing you're selling, whether it's a physical item, like a skateboard, or a service, like tutoring.

- **What makes your product special?**
  To succeed in marketing, you need to clearly understand what makes your product unique. Is it better quality? Does it have features that other products don't? Or maybe it solves a problem no one else has addressed. This is called your **unique selling point** (USP). Your USP is what makes your product stand out from the competition.
- For example, let's say you make phone cases that are not only stylish but also biodegradable, meaning they're eco-friendly and won't harm the planet. That's a unique selling point!
- **Understanding your audience**
  Knowing your product also means understanding who would want to buy it. Are you targeting teenagers who want cool designs? Or maybe you're selling to environmentally conscious adults who care about reducing plastic waste. By understanding who your product is for, you can shape your marketing message to speak directly to them.
- **Key Questions for Product**:
- What is your product or service?
- What makes it different from others on the market?
- Who is your ideal customer?

---

2. Price: How Much Should You Charge?

The second "P" is **Price**. This is how much money you're asking people to pay for your product. Pricing isn't just about covering the costs of making your product—it's also about finding the sweet spot where people feel the price matches the value they're getting.

- **Pricing Strategy**:
  Setting the right price involves several factors. You need to think about how much it costs to make or provide your product and how much people are willing to pay for it. If you charge too much, people might look for cheaper alternatives. If you charge too little, customers might think your product isn't as good as more expensive ones, or you might not make enough profit.
- There are different strategies for pricing:
  - **Competitive Pricing**: Setting your price based on what your competitors charge.
  - **Premium Pricing**: Charging a higher price to make your product seem more exclusive or high-end.
  - **Discount Pricing**: Offering lower prices to attract more customers, especially if your goal is to sell in large quantities.
- **Perception of Value**:
  Price isn't just a number; it tells customers what to expect. If your product is expensive, people might expect it to be high-quality or exclusive. On the other hand, if it's very cheap, they might think it's not well made. You need to match your pricing with the value you're offering.
- **Key Questions for Price**:
- How much does it cost to produce your product?
- What price will your customers be willing to pay?
- How does your price compare to your competitors?

---

3. Place: Where Will You Sell Your Product?

The third "P" is **Place**, which refers to where and how your product is sold. This could be in a physical store, online, or through third-party retailers like Amazon or Etsy.

- **Choosing the Right Place**:
  Your product needs to be available where your target customers shop. If you're selling a product aimed at teenagers, you might want to sell online, since teens are used to buying things through apps or websites. But if you're selling something like handmade goods or specialty items, you might also consider selling at local markets or boutique stores.
- You can sell in different places:
  - **Online**: Websites, social media platforms, and e-commerce sites.
  - **Physical Stores**: Local shops, big retail chains, or your own store.
  - **Third-Party Sellers**: Amazon, Etsy, or other online marketplaces.
- **Distribution Channels**:
  Distribution is how your product gets to the customers. If you're selling a physical product, you'll need to figure out the logistics of getting your product from where it's made to where it will be sold. You might sell directly to customers, or you might sell to retailers who then sell to the public.
- **Key Questions for Place**:
- Where do your customers shop?
- Will you sell online, in stores, or both?
- How will you deliver your product to your customers?

---

4. Promotion: How Will People Know About Your Product?

The fourth "P" is **Promotion**, and it's all about how you spread the word about your product. Promotion involves the tools you use to advertise your product and convince people to buy it.

- **Advertising**:
  This can include online ads, like on Google or social media platforms, as well as traditional ads, like on TV, radio, or billboards. The goal is to get your product in front of as many potential customers as possible. When promoting online, using targeted ads ensures that your message reaches the people who are most likely to be interested in what you're selling.

- **Sales Promotions**:
  These are short-term incentives to encourage people to buy, like discounts, coupons, or special offers. Think about the "buy one, get one free" deals or limited-time sales that create urgency.
- **Public Relations (PR)**:
  PR is about getting people to talk about your product in a positive way. It could involve working with influencers, getting featured in a magazine, or hosting events. The idea is to create a buzz around your product, so people want to check it out.
- **Social Media and Content Marketing**:
  Social media platforms like Instagram, TikTok, and YouTube are great places to promote your product, especially if you're aiming at younger audiences. You can also create content like blog posts or videos that educate people about your product or provide useful tips related to it.
- **Key Questions for Promotion**:
- How will you let people know about your product?
- Which advertising or promotion methods will you use?
- How can you use social media or influencers to promote your product?

Putting the Four P's Together

The Four P's don't work in isolation. They are interconnected, and together, they help form a strong marketing plan. For example, if you raise the price of your product (Price), you might need to make sure people know why it's worth the higher price through targeted promotions (Promotion). Or, if you start selling online instead of just in stores (Place), you'll need to adjust your marketing to focus more on digital channels.

A successful marketing strategy requires a balance of all Four P's, ensuring that they support and reinforce one another to make your product attractive, available, and valuable to your target audience.

The Four P's of marketing—Product, Price, Place, and Promotion—are essential tools for creating a successful business strategy. By understanding and applying these elements, you can ensure your product reaches the right people, at the right price, in the right places, and with the right message.

Marketing may seem complicated, but if you think about it like baking a cake, the Four P's are your ingredients. Get the mix right, and you'll have a winning recipe for business success.

Chapter 5: Defining Your Product and Audience

One of the most important steps in marketing is knowing exactly what you're offering and who you're offering it to. In other words, you need to clearly define your **product** and your **audience**. If you don't know these things, it's like trying to shoot an arrow without knowing where the target is.
In this chapter, we'll break down how to define your product and identify your audience so that you can effectively market your business.

Understanding Your Product: What Are You Selling?

Before you start marketing, you need to have a crystal-clear understanding of your product. The more you know about it, the easier it is to sell. But what does it mean to "understand" your product?

1. **What Problem Does It Solve?**
   Every good product solves a problem or fulfills a need. Think about what your product or service does for the customer. Does it make life easier? Does it provide something they can't get anywhere else? For example, if you're selling custom-made phone cases, the problem you might be solving is giving customers a way to protect their phones while showing off their personal style.
2. **What Makes It Unique?**
   Chances are, you're not the only one selling a similar product. That's why it's important to figure out what makes yours stand out. This is called your **Unique Selling Proposition (USP)**. Maybe your product is cheaper, more durable, or made with eco-friendly materials. Whatever sets you apart from competitors should be highlighted in your marketing.
3. **Understanding Features and Benefits**
   When talking about your product, you need to be clear about its features (what it has) and its benefits (how it helps the customer). For instance, a phone case might have the feature of being waterproof (a fact about the product), but the benefit is that it keeps the phone safe from spills or rain (why the feature is helpful).

Defining Your Target Audience: Who Are You Selling To?

Once you understand your product, the next step is figuring out who will want to buy it. You can't market to everyone—you need to focus on the people most likely to be interested in what you're offering. This is called your **target audience**.

1. **Demographics**
   Demographics are basic characteristics of your audience, such as:
   - **Age**: Are you targeting teenagers, adults, or seniors?
   - **Gender**: Is your product more appealing to men, women, or everyone?
   - **Income**: Are you selling something that requires a certain income level to afford?
   - **Location**: Do you want to focus on local customers or a global market?
2. For example, if you're selling video games, your target audience might be teenagers and young adults, mostly male, and living in countries where gaming is popular.
3. **Psychographics**
   Psychographics go deeper into what your audience likes, dislikes, and cares about. It includes things like:
   - **Interests**: What are their hobbies? Do they like fashion, sports, or technology?
   - **Values**: What do they care about? Are they passionate about the environment, fitness, or luxury goods?
   - **Behavior**: How do they shop? Do they prefer buying online or in stores? Are they bargain hunters, or are they willing to pay more for premium products?
4. For example, if you're selling eco-friendly clothing, your target audience might care a lot about sustainability and be willing to pay more for products that are good for the planet.
5. **Narrowing Down Your Audience**
   It's important not to try to reach too many people at once. The more specific you are, the easier it is to create a message that speaks directly to the people who are most likely to buy from you. Instead of targeting "everyone who likes fashion," you could focus on "women aged 18-30 who love eco-friendly, minimalist clothing."

Why Defining Your Audience Matters

Knowing who your audience is helps you tailor your marketing messages. You wouldn't talk to a group of teenagers the same way you'd talk to business executives, right? Understanding your audience allows you to:

- **Use the right language**: Younger audiences might respond to casual, fun language, while professionals might prefer a more formal tone.
- **Choose the right platforms**: If your target audience is teenagers, you'll want to focus on platforms like TikTok or Instagram. But if you're selling business software, LinkedIn might be a better fit.
- **Design the right product features**: By knowing your audience, you can also refine your product to better meet their needs. For example, if your audience values convenience, you might focus on making your product easier to use.

How to Research Your Audience

You might be wondering, "How do I figure out who my target audience is?" Here are some ways to find out:

1. **Surveys and Questionnaires**
   You can create a simple survey asking people what they like, what problems they need solved, and how they usually shop. This can give you valuable insight into who your customers are.
2. **Analyze Your Competitors**
   Look at businesses similar to yours. Who are they targeting? What type of customers are buying from them? You can learn a lot from observing what's working for other businesses.
3. **Use Social Media and Online Tools**
   Platforms like Instagram, Facebook, and Google Analytics provide tools that help you see who's interacting with your brand. This can give you an idea of your audience's age, location, and interests.
4. **Test and Learn**
   Sometimes the best way to figure out your audience is to test different approaches and see what works. Try running ads targeted at different groups and see which ones respond best.

Creating a Customer Persona

A **customer persona** is a fictional representation of your ideal customer. Think of it as creating a profile of one person who represents your target audience. This makes it easier to tailor your marketing.
For example, let's say you're selling fitness equipment. You might create a persona named "Fit Alex":

- **Age**: 25
- **Occupation**: Office worker
- **Interests**: Staying healthy, working out at the gym, trying new fitness trends
- **Shopping Behavior**: Prefers to buy online, looks for discounts but is willing to spend more for high-quality products
- **Motivation**: Wants to stay in shape and improve health, values convenience and quick results
- By creating this persona, you can design marketing messages that speak directly to "Fit Alex," knowing that many other people in your audience will have similar traits.

Combining Product and Audience

Once you've defined your product and your audience, the next step is to bring them together. Ask yourself, **"Why does my product appeal to this audience?"** This is where you connect the dots between what your product offers and what your audience wants.
For example:

- If your audience is young adults who care about sustainability, you might highlight the eco-friendly materials in your product.
- If your audience is busy professionals, you might emphasize how your product saves them time or makes their life easier.
- By aligning your product with your audience's needs, your marketing will be more effective because it will feel personal and relevant to the people you're targeting.

Defining your product and audience is the foundation of any good marketing strategy. When you understand exactly what you're selling and who you're selling it to, you can create more effective marketing campaigns that speak directly to the people most likely to buy your product. Whether it's through surveys, competitor analysis, or creating customer personas, the more you know about your audience, the better you can serve them. And when your product is aligned with your audience's needs, you're setting your business up for success!

Part 2: Traditional Marketing Strategies

Chapter 6: Outdoor Marketing Techniques

Outdoor marketing is one of the most traditional yet effective ways to promote a business. It involves reaching people when they're outside of their homes—whether they're walking around town, driving, or using public transportation. Even in the digital age, outdoor marketing remains a powerful tool to catch the attention of potential customers.
In this chapter, we'll explore different types of outdoor marketing techniques, how they work, and why they're still relevant today.

What is Outdoor Marketing?

Outdoor marketing refers to any advertising done in public spaces. The idea is to catch people's attention as they go about their day. This type of marketing is often eye-catching and designed to make a strong, quick impression since people are usually on the move when they see it.
Outdoor marketing works best in high-traffic areas where many people are likely to see the advertisement. Some of the most common outdoor marketing techniques include billboards, posters, and transit ads (like bus or train ads).

Types of Outdoor Marketing

Let's break down the main types of outdoor marketing:

1. **Billboards**
    - Billboards are giant advertisements placed in busy locations, like highways or city streets. They are designed to be seen by thousands of people as they drive or walk by. Billboards are often bold and simple, with large images and short messages that can be read quickly.
    - **Example**: Think of the huge Coca-Cola billboard in Times Square that people from all over the world see every day. It's bright, eye-catching, and immediately recognizable.
2. **Transit Advertising**

- Transit advertising includes ads placed on buses, trains, subways, or even taxis. Since many people rely on public transportation, this type of marketing can reach a broad audience.
- **Example**: You've probably seen bus wraps with advertisements covering the entire side of the bus. These large ads move through different neighborhoods, spreading the message to a wide range of people.

3. **Posters and Flyers**
   - Posters and flyers are smaller than billboards but still effective. They can be placed in public areas like coffee shops, community boards, bus stops, and school campuses.
   - **Example**: A local concert promoter might put up posters around town advertising an upcoming show, making sure they're visible to people who like live music.
4. **Street Furniture Advertising**
   - This type of advertising is placed on things like benches, bus shelters, or trash cans. It's a great way to reach people in a specific area, like a busy city center or a neighborhood park.
   - **Example**: A bus shelter ad for a new movie might grab the attention of people waiting for their ride, giving them something to look at while they wait.
5. **Vehicle Wraps**
   - Vehicle wraps involve covering a car, van, or truck with promotional material. It turns the vehicle into a moving billboard, advertising a product or service wherever it goes.
   - **Example**: Delivery vans covered in logos and messages for a flower shop could spread awareness of the business as they drive around delivering flowers.

Why Outdoor Marketing Still Works

Even though many people spend a lot of time online, outdoor marketing continues to be effective. Here are a few reasons why:

1. **Wide Reach**
   - Outdoor ads can reach a huge number of people, especially in busy areas like cities or highways. Unlike social media ads that target specific users, outdoor marketing is more about getting as many eyes on your ad as possible.
2. **High Visibility**

   - Because outdoor ads are often large and bold, they can't be easily ignored. People are likely to notice a big billboard as they drive by, even if they don't stop to read it fully.
3. **Works with Other Marketing Channels**
   - Outdoor marketing often works best when combined with other forms of marketing. For example, seeing a billboard for a new phone might remind someone of an ad they saw online, making them more likely to look up the product later.
4. **Constant Exposure**
   - Unlike a TV or online ad that plays for a few seconds, outdoor ads are visible 24/7. They're always there, reminding people about your product every time they pass by.

Tips for Effective Outdoor Marketing

Outdoor marketing might seem simple, but to get the best results, you need to plan it carefully. Here are some tips to make sure your outdoor marketing hits the mark:

1. **Keep It Simple**
   - Outdoor ads are usually seen quickly, so keep the message short and easy to understand. Use large text and bold images that people can take in at a glance.
   - **Example**: A billboard for a new fast-food restaurant might just say, "Hungry? Try our new burgers!" with a picture of the food and the restaurant's logo.
2. **Choose the Right Location**
   - Make sure your ad is placed where your target audience will see it. If you're advertising a luxury product, you might choose an upscale neighborhood or a downtown shopping area. If it's a more casual product, a high-traffic highway might work better.
   - **Example**: Ads for sportswear might be placed near gyms or parks where fitness enthusiasts are likely to hang out.
3. **Use Eye-Catching Design**
   - Bright colors, bold fonts, and interesting images can help your ad stand out. Don't be afraid to be creative and make your ad visually appealing.
   - **Example**: A vehicle wrap for an ice cream shop might use bright colors and pictures of delicious ice cream cones to attract attention.
4. **Call to Action**

- Even though outdoor ads are brief, they should still include a simple call to action, like "Visit our website" or "Stop by today." This encourages people to take the next step.
- **Example**: A poster for a music festival might include a website URL where people can buy tickets or find more information.

Challenges of Outdoor Marketing

While outdoor marketing has many benefits, it also has some challenges:

1. **Cost**
    - Renting billboard space or wrapping a vehicle can be expensive, especially in high-traffic areas. You'll need to budget carefully and make sure the cost is worth the exposure you'll get.
2. **Limited Message**
    - Because people don't spend a lot of time looking at outdoor ads, you don't have room for long messages. You have to get your point across quickly and clearly, which can be tricky.
3. **Weather and Timing**
    - Outdoor ads are exposed to the elements, so they need to be durable. If the ad is damaged by weather, it might not be as effective. Timing is also important—an ad for a summer event won't work if it's still up when winter comes around.

Outdoor marketing remains an important part of many businesses' advertising strategies. Whether you're using billboards, transit ads, or posters, the goal is to reach people in their everyday lives and create a lasting impression. By keeping your message simple, choosing the right locations, and using eye-catching designs, outdoor marketing can help your business stand out and attract more customers. Even in the digital age, outdoor advertising proves that sometimes the best way to get noticed is by being where people already are—outside, on the move, and ready to take notice.

Chapter 7: Print Marketing

Even though we live in a digital age where social media and online ads seem to dominate, **print marketing** remains a powerful and effective way to reach customers. Print marketing refers to any marketing that involves printed materials like brochures, flyers, and posters. It's especially useful for reaching local customers and creating a tangible connection between the brand and the audience.

In this chapter, we'll explore what print marketing is, the different types of print materials, and how businesses can use them effectively to grow their customer base.

What is Print Marketing?

Print marketing involves the use of physical, printed materials to promote a product, service, or business. These materials can be handed out to people, mailed to their homes, or displayed in public spaces. The goal of print marketing is to grab attention, share information, and encourage people to take action, like visiting a store or making a purchase.

While digital marketing reaches people through their phones and computers, print marketing reaches people when they're offline—at home, walking around town, or even at an event. The physical nature of printed materials can make them feel more personal and harder to ignore than a digital ad.

Types of Print Marketing

There are several types of print marketing materials, each with its own purpose. Let's break down the most common ones:

1. **Flyers**
    - Flyers are small, printed sheets that are easy to hand out or post around town. They usually contain brief information about an event, sale, or new product. Flyers are great for short-term promotions.
    - **Example**: A flyer promoting a local pizza place might include a picture of a delicious pizza, a special discount offer, and the restaurant's phone number and address.
2. **Brochures**

- Brochures are folded pieces of paper that contain more detailed information. Businesses often use brochures to explain their services or products in more depth. They can be handed out at events or left in places where people can pick them up.
- **Example**: A travel agency might use a brochure to showcase different vacation packages, complete with photos, pricing, and a call to book a trip.

3. **Business Cards**
    - Business cards are small cards that include contact information for a business or individual. They're useful for networking, helping people remember who you are and how to reach you later.
    - **Example**: A graphic designer might hand out business cards at a conference, with their name, website, and contact info on it.
4. **Posters**
    - Posters are larger printed materials designed to catch people's attention in public spaces. Posters are typically used to promote events, such as concerts or community festivals.
    - **Example**: A poster for a new movie might be placed in bus shelters or on the walls of a local café to get people excited about the release date.
5. **Catalogs**
    - Catalogs are booklets that showcase a company's products or services. They're often mailed to customers' homes or distributed at events. Catalogs let customers browse through a company's offerings and decide what they want to buy.
    - **Example**: A clothing company might send out a seasonal catalog featuring its latest collection, along with pricing and information on how to order.
6. **Direct Mail**
    - Direct mail refers to any marketing material that is mailed directly to people's homes. This could be postcards, coupons, or small catalogs. Direct mail is highly targeted since businesses usually send it to a specific group of people, like local residents or loyal customers.
    - **Example**: A local gym might send a postcard with a special offer for new memberships to homes in the neighborhood.

Why Print Marketing Still Works

Even though many businesses focus heavily on digital marketing, print marketing still has a lot of advantages:

1. **Tangibility**
    - People can hold and touch printed materials, which makes them feel more real and personal. A digital ad can disappear with a click, but a flyer or brochure can sit on someone's desk or fridge, reminding them of your business.
2. **Targeted Reach**
    - With print marketing, you can target specific locations or groups of people. For example, if you run a local bakery, you can hand out flyers or mail postcards to homes in your area, making sure that your marketing is reaching the people most likely to visit your shop.
3. **Less Competition**
    - Online, people are bombarded with ads on every website, app, and social media platform. In comparison, print marketing often has less competition for attention, especially when placed in the right spots, like community boards or mailboxes.
4. **Longer Shelf Life**
    - Unlike a digital ad that disappears after a few seconds, print materials can stick around for a while. A well-designed brochure or poster might be kept for future reference, giving your business long-term exposure.

Tips for Effective Print Marketing

To make sure your print marketing materials are effective, you need to follow some important guidelines:

1. **Design Matters**
    - First impressions are everything. Your print materials should look professional and visually appealing. Use bright colors, clear fonts, and high-quality images to grab attention. Make sure the design reflects your brand's personality.
    - **Example**: A high-end spa might use soft, calming colors and elegant fonts to convey a sense of luxury, while a skate shop might use bold, energetic colors to appeal to a younger crowd.
2. **Keep It Simple**

- Don't overload your print materials with too much information. People should be able to understand the main message quickly. Include only the most important details, like what you're offering and how people can contact or visit you.
- **Example**: A flyer for a summer sale should focus on the dates of the sale, the discount being offered, and the location of the store—no need for long paragraphs of text.

3. **Call to Action**
   - Every print material should include a clear **call to action** (CTA), which tells people what to do next. Whether it's "Visit our website," "Call now to book an appointment," or "Use this coupon for 20% off," your CTA should make it easy for people to take the next step.
   - **Example**: A postcard from a local dentist might say, "Call today for a free consultation!" along with the phone number and office hours.
4. **Track Your Results**
   - It's important to know whether your print marketing is working. You can do this by including things like special coupon codes, QR codes, or trackable phone numbers. This way, you'll know how many people responded to your print campaign.
   - **Example**: A café might include a coupon code on its flyers that people can use when ordering online. The number of times the code is used will show how effective the flyer campaign was.

Challenges of Print Marketing

While print marketing has many benefits, it also comes with a few challenges:

1. **Cost**
   - Printing materials like brochures and posters can be expensive, especially if you need a large quantity. Plus, you'll need to pay for distribution—whether that's mailing the materials or hiring people to hand them out.
2. **No Instant Feedback**
   - Unlike digital marketing, where you can immediately see how many people clicked on an ad, print marketing doesn't provide instant feedback. It can take time to see if your efforts are working.
3. **Limited Reach**

  - Print marketing usually focuses on local areas, which means it might not be the best option if you're trying to reach a wider, more global audience.

Combining Print and Digital Marketing

One of the best ways to make print marketing even more effective is to combine it with digital marketing. This gives you the best of both worlds—print materials grab people's attention offline, while digital marketing helps you reach them online.

- **Use QR Codes**: Include QR codes on your print materials that lead people to your website, social media pages, or online store. This helps bridge the gap between offline and online marketing.
  - **Example**: A restaurant could print a QR code on its flyer that, when scanned, takes customers directly to the menu on its website.
- **Promote Your Social Media**: Add your social media handles to your print materials so people know where to find you online.
  - **Example**: A clothing store's catalog might include links to its Instagram and TikTok pages, encouraging people to follow for the latest styles and updates.
- **Track Your Print Campaigns**: As mentioned earlier, using coupon codes or special URLs can help track how many people engage with your print marketing through online channels.
  - **Example**: A gym could include a URL on its direct mail postcards that leads to a special sign-up page for new members.

Print marketing may be one of the oldest forms of advertising, but it's far from outdated. When done right, it can make a big impact, especially when targeting local customers or promoting special events. By using high-quality design, clear messaging, and combining print with digital marketing, businesses can create memorable campaigns that reach their audience in a personal and effective way.

Whether it's handing out flyers at a local event or mailing brochures to potential customers, print marketing gives your brand a physical presence in the real world, helping you connect with people in ways that digital ads sometimes can't.

Chapter 8: Direct Marketing Strategies

Direct marketing is one of the oldest and most effective ways for businesses to communicate directly with their customers. It involves reaching out to people individually, often through personalized messages, with the goal of getting them to take action, like making a purchase or signing up for a service. Direct marketing is powerful because it speaks to people in a personal way, making them feel like the business cares specifically about them.

In this chapter, we'll explore different types of direct marketing strategies, how they work, and why they're still important in today's world.

What is Direct Marketing?

Direct marketing is all about **communicating directly with the customer**. Unlike other marketing strategies that use broad messages aimed at a large audience (like TV commercials or billboards), direct marketing targets individuals or small groups. The idea is to get a quick response, like making a sale or getting someone to join a mailing list.

Direct marketing can take many forms, such as emails, text messages, phone calls, and even direct mail (like postcards or catalogs). What makes it "direct" is that the message goes straight to the customer without any middleman, like an ad on TV or in a magazine.

Types of Direct Marketing

There are several popular types of direct marketing, and each one has its own strengths. Let's go through the most common ones:

1. **Email Marketing**
    - Email marketing involves sending promotional messages, newsletters, or special offers to people's inboxes. This is one of the most common forms of direct marketing because almost everyone has an email address, and it's inexpensive to send large volumes of emails.
    - **Example**: A clothing store might send an email to customers offering a 20% discount on their next purchase if they shop online within the next week.
2. **SMS/Text Message Marketing**

- SMS marketing sends promotional messages directly to customers' phones through text messages. It's quick, personal, and highly effective because most people check their phones regularly.
- **Example**: A restaurant might send a text message to customers letting them know about a special deal for lunch that day, encouraging them to stop by.

3. **Direct Mail**
   - Direct mail is the practice of sending physical marketing materials like postcards, catalogs, or letters to people's homes. Even in the digital age, direct mail can be very effective, especially when it includes special offers or personalized messages.
   - **Example**: A local car dealership might send a postcard to nearby residents with details about a weekend sale, including a coupon for a discount on car services.
4. **Telemarketing**
   - Telemarketing involves calling potential customers on the phone to tell them about a product or service. While some people find telemarketing annoying, it can still be effective, especially when targeting a specific group of people who might be interested in the offer.
   - **Example**: A home security company might call homeowners in a specific area to offer a free home security consultation.
5. **Social Media Direct Messaging (DMs)**
   - Many businesses are now using social media to reach out to customers through direct messages on platforms like Instagram, Facebook, or Twitter. This allows companies to have one-on-one conversations with potential customers, answer their questions, and make personalized offers.
   - **Example**: A beauty brand might send a direct message to someone who follows them on Instagram, offering a discount code for their first purchase.

Why Direct Marketing is Effective

Direct marketing works for several reasons, and businesses love it because it leads to **quick and measurable results**. Here's why it's so effective:

1. **Personalization**

- One of the biggest advantages of direct marketing is that it can be personalized. When businesses send personalized messages—like using a customer's name or referencing past purchases—it makes the customer feel valued and more likely to respond.
- **Example**: "Hi Sarah! We noticed you loved our eco-friendly sneakers. For a limited time, enjoy 15% off your next purchase."

2. **Targeted Audience**
   - Direct marketing allows businesses to target specific groups of people who are most likely to be interested in their product or service. Instead of wasting time and money advertising to everyone, they focus on the people who are most likely to respond.
   - **Example**: A pet supply company might send emails only to customers who have previously purchased dog food, offering them a discount on a new line of dog toys.
3. **Immediate Feedback**
   - Because direct marketing often leads to quick responses, businesses can quickly see if their campaign is working. For example, they can track how many people clicked a link in an email or used a coupon they received in the mail.
   - **Example**: If a gym sends out a special offer for a free week of membership, they can track how many people sign up and see if the campaign is successful.
4. **Cost-Effective**
   - Direct marketing, especially through email or text messages, is relatively cheap compared to other forms of marketing. There's no need to pay for expensive TV commercials or magazine ads, and businesses can still reach a lot of people with a small budget.
   - **Example**: A local coffee shop might send text messages to 500 customers with a special offer for a free drink, which costs much less than printing flyers or paying for a radio ad.

Tips for Successful Direct Marketing

To get the most out of direct marketing, businesses need to follow a few key strategies. Here's how to make direct marketing campaigns as effective as possible:

1. **Segment Your Audience**

- Not every customer is the same, so it's important to divide (or segment) your audience into groups based on things like their age, location, or purchase history. This way, you can send each group more relevant messages.
- **Example**: A music streaming service might send different emails to customers who listen to pop music and those who prefer rock, offering recommendations based on their preferences.

2. **Create Clear and Engaging Messages**
   - Direct marketing messages need to be clear and to the point. Since people get a lot of emails and texts every day, it's important to grab their attention quickly. Use bold headlines, simple language, and make the offer easy to understand.
   - **Example**: "Get 25% off your next order—Shop now!" This kind of message is short, clear, and encourages the customer to take action.
3. **Include a Strong Call to Action (CTA)**
   - Every direct marketing message should have a strong **Call to Action** (CTA). A CTA tells the customer what you want them to do next, like "Click here to buy now" or "Call today for a free consultation."
   - **Example**: An email from a fitness center might include the CTA: "Sign up today and get your first month free! Click here to join now."
4. **Follow Up**
   - Sometimes, people don't respond to the first message, but that doesn't mean they're not interested. Following up with a reminder message can encourage them to take action. Just make sure not to spam them with too many messages.
   - **Example**: A furniture store might send a reminder email a few days after a sale starts, saying, "Hurry! Our sale ends tomorrow—don't miss out on 30% off all sofas."

Challenges of Direct Marketing

While direct marketing is effective, it does come with some challenges:

1. **Privacy Concerns**
   - People are becoming more concerned about their privacy, and they don't always like receiving unsolicited messages. Businesses need to be careful not to overstep boundaries and should make sure they have permission to contact customers.

- **Example**: Before sending marketing emails, companies should ask customers to opt-in (or agree) to receive messages.

2. **Overload**
   - Many people receive dozens of marketing messages every day, which means they can become overwhelmed and start ignoring them. It's important for businesses to make their messages stand out.
   - **Example**: Instead of sending generic emails, a company might send personalized offers or limited-time deals to grab attention.

Combining Direct Marketing with Digital Marketing

Direct marketing works best when combined with other forms of digital marketing, like social media or online advertising. Here's how businesses can blend the two:

1. **Email and Social Media**
   - A business could send an email promoting a new product and include links to their social media pages for more details or behind-the-scenes content.
   - **Example**: A makeup brand might send an email about a new product launch and encourage customers to check out a live tutorial on Instagram.
2. **Text Messages and Online Shopping**
   - Text messages could include direct links to online shopping pages, making it easy for customers to buy products with just a few taps on their phones.
   - **Example**: A sneaker store could send a text message with a link to its online store, offering free shipping for the next 24 hours.

Direct marketing remains a valuable tool for businesses because it allows them to connect with customers in a personal, targeted way. Whether through emails, text messages, direct mail, or phone calls, direct marketing encourages quick responses and builds stronger relationships with customers.

By using clear messages, personalized offers, and strong calls to action, businesses can see real results from their direct marketing efforts. And by combining direct marketing with other digital marketing strategies, companies can create even more effective campaigns that reach people wherever they are—whether in their inbox, on their phone, or through their mailbox.

Chapter 9: Event Marketing

Event marketing is all about creating experiences for your customers that bring them face-to-face with your brand. Whether it's a product launch, a trade show, a community event, or even an online webinar, events give businesses the opportunity to connect directly with their target audience in a meaningful way. Event marketing can help build relationships, raise brand awareness, and create excitement around a product or service.

In this chapter, we'll dive into the different types of event marketing, why it's such a powerful tool, and how businesses can use it effectively to grow their customer base.

What is Event Marketing?

Event marketing involves promoting a brand, product, or service through a live or virtual event. These events are designed to engage people, give them hands-on experiences, and build a stronger connection between the audience and the business. Unlike other forms of marketing that are more passive (like watching a TV ad or seeing a billboard), event marketing is interactive and often allows customers to experience the product or service firsthand.

Types of Event Marketing

There are many different ways businesses can use events to promote their products and services. Here are some of the most common types of event marketing:

1. **Product Launch Events**
    - These are events specifically designed to introduce a new product or service to the public. They are often used to create excitement and generate buzz around the launch. Product launch events can be held in person or online, depending on the size of the audience.
    - **Example**: When Apple releases a new iPhone, they hold a big event where they demonstrate all the new features and invite journalists and influencers to check it out.
2. **Trade Shows and Expos**

- Trade shows and expos bring together businesses from a particular industry to showcase their products and services. These events are usually attended by potential customers, business partners, and industry experts, making them a great place to network and build relationships.
- **Example**: A company that sells fitness equipment might set up a booth at a fitness expo where people can try out the machines and ask questions.

3. **Workshops and Seminars**
    - Workshops and seminars are educational events that allow businesses to share their knowledge and expertise with attendees. These events are typically smaller and more focused, giving businesses a chance to provide valuable information while also promoting their products or services.
    - **Example**: A marketing agency might host a seminar on social media strategies, where attendees learn new skills and see how the agency can help them.
4. **Community Events**
    - Community events are local gatherings that bring businesses and residents together. These events help businesses connect with their local audience and build a stronger relationship with the community. They might include things like charity runs, festivals, or local fairs.
    - **Example**: A bakery might sponsor a local food festival where they hand out free samples of their pastries to attract new customers.
5. **Webinars and Virtual Events**
    - Virtual events, like webinars or online conferences, have become increasingly popular, especially since they allow businesses to reach a global audience without the need for physical space. These events are hosted online and can include presentations, live demonstrations, and Q&A sessions.
    - **Example**: A software company might host a webinar to demonstrate the features of its new app and answer questions from potential users around the world.

Why Event Marketing is Powerful

Event marketing is effective because it gives customers a chance to interact with a brand in a more personal and direct way. Here are a few reasons why event marketing works so well:

1. **Building Personal Connections**
   - Events allow businesses to interact with their audience in real-time, which helps build trust and a personal connection. When customers meet the people behind the brand and see the product up close, they're more likely to feel a stronger attachment to the business.
   - **Example**: At a pop-up shop for a clothing brand, customers might meet the designer and learn about the story behind the brand, making them feel more connected to the clothes they buy.
2. **Creating Memorable Experiences**
   - Events are unique because they create memorable experiences for attendees. Unlike a TV ad that people forget after a few seconds, a fun or exciting event sticks with people for a long time. This makes them more likely to remember the brand and talk about it with others.
   - **Example**: A car company might set up a test-driving event where potential customers can take the latest models for a spin, creating a memorable hands-on experience.
3. **Generating Buzz and Excitement**
   - Events are great for generating excitement and buzz, especially when they involve a product launch or a big announcement. People love being part of something exclusive, and they'll often share their experiences on social media, which helps spread the word even further.
   - **Example**: A tech company might create a countdown to a big event, building suspense and excitement among fans who are eager to see the new product.
4. **Getting Immediate Feedback**
   - Events give businesses the chance to get immediate feedback from customers. Whether it's a product demonstration or a live Q&A, businesses can learn what people think and use that information to improve their offerings.

- **Example**: A video game company might host a demo event where players can try out a new game and give feedback on the gameplay, helping the company make adjustments before the official release.

How to Plan a Successful Event

Planning a successful event takes time and effort, but with the right approach, it can be a highly rewarding way to market your business. Here are some steps to ensure your event runs smoothly and achieves your goals:

1. **Set Clear Goals**
   - Before planning the event, decide what you want to achieve. Is your goal to increase brand awareness? Generate sales? Launch a new product? Having clear goals will guide your decisions as you plan the event.
   - **Example**: If your goal is to launch a new product, you'll want to focus on showcasing its features and giving people a chance to try it out.
2. **Choose the Right Audience**
   - Your event should target the people most likely to be interested in your product or service. Whether it's a small, exclusive group of influencers or a large public gathering, make sure you invite the right audience.
   - **Example**: If you're launching a new skincare line, you might want to invite beauty influencers and skincare enthusiasts who will share their experiences with their followers.
3. **Pick a Great Location**
   - The location of your event plays a big role in its success. If it's an in-person event, choose a venue that's accessible and suits the theme of your event. For virtual events, make sure the platform you're using is easy to navigate and can handle the number of attendees.
   - **Example**: A tech company might choose a modern, high-tech venue for their product launch to match the sleek design of their products.
4. **Create Engaging Content**

- Make sure your event is engaging and fun for attendees. This could include live demonstrations, interactive activities, giveaways, or even live entertainment. The more engaged your audience is, the more likely they are to remember your brand and take action.
- **Example**: A fitness brand might host a workout class at their event, allowing attendees to use their products and see how effective they are.

5. **Promote Your Event**
    - For your event to be successful, you need to make sure people know about it. Use social media, email marketing, and even traditional advertising to spread the word. If it's a virtual event, make it easy for people to sign up online.
    - **Example**: A restaurant hosting a grand opening event might promote it on Instagram, offering a sneak peek at the menu and encouraging followers to RSVP for a special discount.

Post-Event Follow-Up

After your event is over, the work isn't done yet! It's important to follow up with attendees to keep the connection going and turn their interest into action. Here's how you can do that:

1. **Send a Thank-You Message**
    - A simple thank-you email or social media message to attendees can go a long way in building goodwill. It shows that you appreciate their time and encourages them to stay connected with your brand.
    - **Example**: After a webinar, a software company might send attendees a thank-you email with a link to watch a recording of the presentation.
2. **Share Event Highlights**
    - Sharing photos or videos from the event can help keep the momentum going and give people who couldn't attend a glimpse of what they missed. This can encourage people to attend your next event.
    - **Example**: A fashion brand might post photos from their runway show on social media, tagging attendees and influencers who were there.
3. **Offer Special Deals**

- To keep the excitement alive, you can offer exclusive deals or promotions to event attendees. This encourages them to make a purchase or sign up for a service after the event is over.
- **Example**: A fitness studio might offer a 10% discount on memberships to everyone who attended their grand opening event.

Challenges of Event Marketing

While event marketing can be incredibly effective, it also comes with challenges. Here are a few things to watch out for:

1. **High Costs**
    - Hosting events, especially in-person ones, can be expensive. You'll need to budget for things like venue rental, equipment, food, and marketing materials. It's important to weigh the potential return on investment to make sure the cost is worth it.
2. **Logistical Complications**
    - Planning and running an event involves a lot of moving parts. There's always the chance that something could go wrong, from a technical issue with a virtual event to a last-minute venue problem. Having a backup plan is always a good idea.

Part 3: Digital Marketing Essentials

Chapter 10: Search Engine Marketing (SEM)

In today's world, almost everyone uses search engines like Google to find information, products, and services. This is why **Search Engine Marketing (SEM)** is such an important part of any business's marketing strategy. SEM helps businesses show up at the top of search results when people are looking for things online, making it easier to attract potential customers.
In this chapter, we'll explore what SEM is, how it works, and why it's such a powerful tool for businesses. We'll also cover some important tips for using SEM effectively to drive traffic to your website.

What is Search Engine Marketing (SEM)?

SEM is a type of digital marketing that focuses on getting your business to show up in search engine results when people search for certain keywords. There are two main types of SEM:

1. **Paid Search Ads (PPC)**
   - The most common form of SEM is **Pay-Per-Click (PPC)** advertising. With PPC, businesses pay to have their ads show up at the top of search engine results. These are the ads you see when you search for something on Google, usually marked with a small "Ad" label.
   - The way it works is simple: Businesses bid on keywords related to their product or service. When someone searches for that keyword, the search engine shows the highest bidders' ads at the top of the results page. The business only pays if someone actually clicks on the ad.
2. **Organic Search (SEO)**

  - While PPC is a paid form of SEM, there's also **Search Engine Optimization (SEO)**, which is about improving your website's content so that it ranks higher in search results naturally (without paying for ads). SEO is a long-term strategy focused on making your website more attractive to search engines by using relevant keywords, improving site performance, and creating high-quality content.
3. While SEO is a free way to get your site noticed, it takes time to see results. PPC, on the other hand, can give businesses immediate visibility but costs money.

Why SEM is Important

SEM is one of the most effective ways to get people to visit your website. Here's why it matters so much:

1. **People Trust Search Engines**
   - Most people use search engines like Google when they're looking for products, services, or information. If your business doesn't show up in the search results, you're missing out on a huge opportunity to reach potential customers.
2. **It Targets People Ready to Buy**
   - One of the best things about SEM is that it targets people who are already interested in what you're offering. When someone searches for a product or service, it's because they need or want it. This means they're more likely to click on your ad and make a purchase.
3. **Quick Results with PPC**
   - While SEO takes time to show results, PPC can get your business in front of customers immediately. As soon as your ad goes live, it starts showing up in search results, and you can start getting clicks right away.
4. **You Only Pay for Results**
   - With PPC, you only pay when someone clicks on your ad. This means you're not wasting money on people who aren't interested. It's a cost-effective way to make sure you're only paying for actual visitors to your site.

How PPC Works

Let's dive a bit deeper into how PPC works. PPC is an auction system where businesses bid on specific keywords that they want their ads to show up for. The search engine (like Google) looks at all the bids and decides whose ad to show based on two main factors:

1. **Bid Amount**
    - This is the amount of money a business is willing to pay for each click on their ad. The higher the bid, the more likely the ad will show up at the top of the search results.
2. **Ad Quality and Relevance**
    - Google and other search engines don't just look at the bid amount—they also care about how relevant and high-quality the ad is. This includes things like how well the ad matches the search term, how good the ad's copy is, and how useful the landing page is (the page the ad links to).
    - If an ad is more relevant to the searcher's query, it can still win the auction even if the bid is lower than other businesses.

Tips for Running a Successful PPC Campaign

Running a successful PPC campaign takes careful planning and strategy. Here are some important tips to keep in mind:

1. **Choose the Right Keywords**
    - The key to a successful PPC campaign is choosing the right keywords. These are the words or phrases people type into search engines when they're looking for something. You need to think like your customers and choose keywords that are relevant to what they would search for.
    - **Example**: If you run a pizza restaurant, your keywords might include "pizza delivery near me" or "best pizza in [city]."
2. **Write Compelling Ads**
    - Your ad needs to stand out from the competition and grab people's attention. The headline should be clear, the offer should be attractive, and there should be a strong **call to action** (CTA), like "Order now" or "Get 20% off today."
    - **Example**: "Hungry? Get 10% off your first order of delicious pizza – order online now!"
3. **Set a Budget**

- With PPC, you decide how much you're willing to spend each day or each month. It's important to set a budget that works for you and adjust it based on how well your ads are performing. Don't spend more than you're comfortable with, especially if you're just starting out.

4. **Track Your Results**
   - One of the biggest advantages of PPC is that you can easily track how well your ads are doing. You can see how many people clicked on your ad, how much you're paying per click, and whether those clicks are turning into sales. Use this information to improve your ads and make them more effective.
   - **Example**: If you notice that a lot of people are clicking on your ad but not making a purchase, you might want to change the landing page to make it more user-friendly.
5. **Use Negative Keywords**
   - Negative keywords are words you don't want your ad to show up for. This helps you avoid paying for clicks from people who aren't interested in your product. For example, if you're selling high-end shoes, you might use "cheap" as a negative keyword so your ad doesn't show up when people search for "cheap shoes."

Understanding SEO: The Organic Side of SEM

While PPC gets quick results, SEO is all about building long-term success. SEO is the process of optimizing your website to rank higher in search engine results without paying for ads. Here's how SEO works:

- **Use Relevant Keywords**
  - Just like with PPC, SEO starts with keywords. You need to use relevant keywords throughout your website, including in titles, headings, and the body of your content. This helps search engines understand what your site is about and rank it higher in search results.
- **Create High-Quality Content**
  - Search engines love websites that offer useful, high-quality content. By creating helpful blog posts, product descriptions, and articles, you can attract more visitors and improve your SEO ranking.
  - **Example**: A pet store might write a blog post about "The Best Toys for Puppies" to attract pet owners looking for advice.

- **Optimize Your Website's Performance**
    - Search engines also consider how well your website performs. This includes things like how fast it loads, how easy it is to navigate, and whether it works well on mobile devices. A slow or confusing website can hurt your SEO ranking.
- **Build Backlinks**
    - Backlinks are links from other websites that point to your site. The more high-quality websites that link to your content, the more search engines trust your site, and the higher it will rank in search results.
    - **Example**: If a popular blog writes an article about your product and links back to your site, that backlink can boost your SEO.

Challenges of SEM

While SEM is incredibly powerful, it does come with some challenges:

1. **Cost**
    - PPC can be expensive, especially in competitive industries where many businesses are bidding on the same keywords. If you're not careful, costs can add up quickly without delivering enough results.
2. **Learning Curve**
    - SEM, especially SEO, can take time to learn. SEO requires patience, as it can take months to see the results of your efforts, while PPC requires a good understanding of how bidding and keywords work.
3. **Constant Monitoring**
    - Both PPC and SEO need to be monitored regularly. PPC campaigns require constant adjustments to make sure you're getting a good return on your investment, and SEO needs to be updated to keep up with changing search engine algorithms.

Search Engine Marketing (SEM) is a must-have tool for any business looking to grow its online presence and attract more customers. Whether you're using paid search ads (PPC) for quick results or focusing on organic search (SEO) for long-term success, SEM allows you to reach people who are actively searching for what you offer.

By choosing the right keywords, creating high-quality content, and keeping a close eye on your campaign performance, you can build an SEM strategy that brings more traffic to your website and helps your business grow. And remember, it's all about finding the right balance between PPC and SEO to meet your business's needs.

Chapter 11: Email Marketing

Email marketing is one of the most powerful and cost-effective ways to communicate directly with your customers. It involves sending emails to people who have shown interest in your business, offering them updates, promotions, and valuable content that encourages them to engage with your brand. In today's digital world, mastering email marketing can help businesses build relationships, increase sales, and keep customers coming back.
In this chapter, we'll cover how email marketing works, why it's important, and the best strategies for running successful email campaigns.

What is Email Marketing?

Email marketing is a digital marketing strategy where businesses send messages, offers, or newsletters to a list of people who have opted to receive communication from them. It's different from spam because the people receiving the emails have agreed to be on your list, meaning they're interested in what your business has to offer.
The goal of email marketing is to maintain regular contact with your audience, keep them informed about your products or services, and encourage them to take action, like making a purchase or signing up for an event.

Why Email Marketing is Important

1. **Direct Access to Your Audience**
    - Unlike social media or paid ads, email marketing allows you to speak directly to your customers. When someone opens your email, they're focused only on what you're saying. This direct connection can lead to stronger relationships and more conversions (sales or actions).
2. **Cost-Effective**
    - Email marketing is one of the most affordable ways to reach a large audience. With the right strategy, you can send thousands of emails for a low cost, making it especially useful for small businesses that don't have huge marketing budgets.
3. **Personalized Communication**

- Emails can be highly personalized, from addressing the recipient by their name to tailoring content based on their previous purchases or preferences. Personalized emails perform better because they feel more relevant to the recipient.
- **Example**: If a customer recently bought a book from an online store, the business could send an email suggesting similar books they might enjoy.

4. **Measurable Results**
    - Email marketing tools provide detailed reports on how many people opened your email, clicked on links, or made purchases. This data helps you understand what works and what doesn't so you can improve your future campaigns.

Types of Emails You Can Send

There are several types of email marketing campaigns you can use to engage your audience. Each one serves a different purpose:

1. **Newsletters**
    - Newsletters are regular emails sent to your subscribers, usually weekly or monthly, that share updates about your business, such as new products, special events, or blog posts. They help keep your brand top of mind.
    - **Example**: A fitness center might send a monthly newsletter with tips on healthy living, upcoming classes, and member success stories.
2. **Promotional Emails**
    - Promotional emails are designed to encourage recipients to take advantage of a special offer, like a discount, sale, or limited-time deal. They create a sense of urgency and often include a call-to-action (CTA) like "Shop Now" or "Claim Your Discount."
    - **Example**: An online store might send an email offering a 20% discount on all items for a weekend sale.
3. **Transactional Emails**
    - Transactional emails are triggered by specific actions a customer takes, such as making a purchase or signing up for an account. They usually include details like order confirmations, shipping updates, or account information.

- **Example**: After a customer buys something online, they receive a confirmation email with their order details and tracking number.

4. **Welcome Emails**
   - Welcome emails are the first emails a new subscriber receives after joining your email list. These emails thank the subscriber for signing up and introduce them to your business, often with a special offer to encourage their first purchase.
   - **Example**: A clothing brand might send a welcome email to new subscribers with a 10% off coupon for their first purchase.
5. **Re-engagement Emails**
   - Re-engagement emails are sent to subscribers who haven't interacted with your emails for a while. These emails are meant to win back their attention and remind them of what your business has to offer.
   - **Example**: A beauty company might send a re-engagement email to customers who haven't made a purchase in six months, offering a special deal to encourage them to return.

Best Practices for Email Marketing

To get the most out of your email marketing efforts, it's important to follow a few key strategies:

1. **Build a Quality Email List**
   - Your email list should be made up of people who are genuinely interested in your business. Avoid buying email lists, as those people are unlikely to engage with your emails and might mark them as spam. Instead, grow your list organically by encouraging people to sign up on your website or during the checkout process.
   - **Example**: A coffee shop could offer a free coffee to customers who sign up for their email list.
2. **Write Compelling Subject Lines**
   - The subject line is the first thing people see in their inbox, so it needs to grab their attention and make them want to open the email. Keep it short, interesting, and relevant to what's inside the email.
   - **Example**: "Your 20% Off Deal is Waiting!" or "5 Easy Ways to Boost Your Workout."
3. **Use Clear Calls-to-Action (CTAs)**

- Every email should have a clear goal, like encouraging people to make a purchase, read a blog post, or sign up for an event. Make sure your CTA is easy to spot and action-oriented, like "Shop Now" or "Get Started."
- **Example**: An email promoting a new product might include a big button that says, "Buy Now."

4. **Segment Your Audience**
   - Not all of your subscribers are interested in the same things. Segmenting your email list into groups based on factors like age, location, or purchase history allows you to send more targeted and relevant emails.
   - **Example**: A travel company might send different emails to customers who prefer beach vacations and those who like mountain adventures.
5. **Mobile-Friendly Design**
   - Many people read emails on their phones, so it's important to make sure your emails look good on mobile devices. Use simple designs, large fonts, and clear CTAs that are easy to click on a small screen.
6. **Test and Improve**
   - Email marketing is not a one-size-fits-all strategy. You should constantly test different subject lines, designs, and CTAs to see what works best. Tools like A/B testing allow you to send different versions of an email to small groups to see which one performs better.

Challenges of Email Marketing

While email marketing has many benefits, it also comes with a few challenges:

1. **Avoiding the Spam Folder**
   - If too many people mark your emails as spam, they may stop reaching your audience altogether. Make sure to only send emails to people who have opted in and avoid sending too many emails in a short period.
2. **Unsubscribes**
   - Over time, some people may unsubscribe from your email list, especially if they feel like they're receiving too many emails or if the content is no longer relevant to them. Keep your emails valuable and space them out to avoid overwhelming your audience.

3. **Competition for Attention**
   - People receive dozens of emails every day, so it can be hard to stand out in a crowded inbox. This is why it's so important to write compelling subject lines and offer content that's interesting and relevant to your subscribers.

Email marketing is an essential tool for any business looking to build strong relationships with its customers and drive sales. By sending the right types of emails, personalizing your content, and following best practices like segmenting your audience and testing your campaigns, you can create emails that people look forward to receiving.

With careful planning and execution, email marketing can help you stay connected with your audience, encourage repeat business, and grow your brand in a meaningful way.

Chapter 12: Social Media Marketing

In today's world, social media has become one of the most important platforms for marketing. Social media marketing is all about using platforms like Instagram, TikTok, Facebook, Twitter, and YouTube to connect with customers, build your brand, and promote products or services. It's a way to reach people where they already spend a lot of time—on their phones, tablets, and computers.

In this chapter, we'll dive into what social media marketing is, why it's so effective, and how businesses can use it to build an engaged audience.

What is Social Media Marketing?

Social media marketing refers to the use of social media platforms to connect with your audience to build your brand, increase sales, and drive website traffic. This involves creating content like posts, videos, and stories that engage followers and encourage them to interact with your brand.

Unlike traditional marketing (like TV ads or print media), social media marketing allows businesses to engage directly with customers. You can have real conversations, answer questions, and get immediate feedback on what your audience thinks about your products or services.

Why Social Media Marketing is So Powerful

1. **Huge Audience**
    - Billions of people use social media every day. This makes it one of the biggest and most powerful tools for reaching potential customers. No matter what kind of business you have, chances are your customers are on at least one social media platform.
2. **Direct Interaction**
    - Social media allows businesses to interact directly with their audience. You can reply to comments, answer questions, and have conversations with your followers in real-time. This builds stronger relationships and shows that you care about your customers.
    - **Example**: A clothing brand might respond to a customer's comment asking about sizing or availability, making the customer feel heard and valued.
3. **Content Sharing**

- Social media makes it easy for people to share your content. If a follower likes your post, they can share it with their friends and family, helping you reach an even larger audience.
- **Example**: A cool, funny video about a new product might be shared hundreds or even thousands of times, giving your brand free exposure.

4. **Targeted Advertising**
   - Social media platforms like Facebook and Instagram allow businesses to create highly targeted ads. You can choose who sees your ads based on factors like age, location, interests, and behaviors. This makes your ads more effective because they're shown to people who are more likely to be interested in your product.
   - **Example**: A skateboard brand might run ads specifically targeting teenagers and young adults who follow skateboarding-related accounts or live in urban areas.
5. **Building Brand Loyalty**
   - When businesses regularly post engaging and helpful content, they build a loyal following. People will start to see your brand as a part of their lives, not just as a company trying to sell them something.
   - **Example**: A fitness brand might post daily workout tips or motivational quotes, encouraging people to stay engaged with the brand even when they're not buying anything.

Popular Social Media Platforms for Marketing

There are many social media platforms, and each one has its own unique audience and style. Let's look at some of the most popular platforms and how businesses can use them:

1. **Instagram**
   - Instagram is a visual platform where users share photos and videos. It's a great place for businesses to showcase products, share behind-the-scenes content, and engage with followers through stories and reels.
   - **Example**: A makeup brand might post tutorials on Instagram, showing how to use their products in creative ways. They could also use Instagram stories to give followers a sneak peek of new product launches.
2. **TikTok**

- TikTok is known for short, entertaining videos that can quickly go viral. It's especially popular with younger audiences, making it a great platform for businesses targeting teens and young adults.
- **Example**: A snack brand might create fun, humorous videos about their products, using popular TikTok trends and challenges to get more views.

3. **Facebook**
   - Facebook is a more traditional social media platform that allows businesses to share posts, images, videos, and ads. It's also a great platform for creating communities through Facebook Groups.
   - **Example**: A gardening supply store might run ads promoting its latest products and create a Facebook Group where members can share gardening tips and ask questions.
4. **YouTube**
   - YouTube is the top platform for video content. Businesses can create videos about their products, how-to guides, or even vlog-style content that helps people connect with the brand on a more personal level.
   - **Example**: A tech company might create YouTube videos demonstrating how to use their products or showcasing customer testimonials.
5. **Twitter**
   - Twitter is a platform for short, text-based posts. It's great for sharing news, updates, and interacting with followers through quick conversations.
   - **Example**: A restaurant might use Twitter to announce daily specials, respond to customer reviews, or engage with food bloggers and influencers.

Strategies for Successful Social Media Marketing

To get the most out of social media marketing, businesses need a clear strategy. Here are some tips for building a successful social media presence:

1. **Create Engaging Content**
   - The key to social media is posting content that grabs people's attention and encourages them to interact with your brand. This could include photos, videos, polls, or stories that are interesting and fun.

  - **Example**: A fashion brand might post a "behind the scenes" video of how their clothes are made or a poll asking followers to vote on their favorite new designs.

2. **Be Consistent**
   - Posting regularly helps keep your audience engaged and reminds them about your brand. Consistency is key—whether that's posting every day, every week, or whatever schedule works best for your business.
   - **Example**: A local bakery might post daily photos of freshly baked goods or share weekly recipes to keep followers excited about their offerings.
3. **Use Hashtags**
   - Hashtags are a way to categorize your posts and make them easier for people to find. Using popular or trending hashtags can help your content reach a wider audience beyond just your followers.
   - **Example**: A travel company might use hashtags like #TravelGoals or #AdventureTime when posting about their vacation packages, making it easier for people interested in travel to discover their posts.
4. **Engage with Your Audience**
   - Social media isn't just about posting—it's about having conversations. Reply to comments, answer questions, and engage with your followers to build stronger relationships.
   - **Example**: A coffee shop might respond to comments on their posts or even repost photos taken by customers enjoying their coffee.
5. **Run Contests and Giveaways**
   - Contests and giveaways are great ways to boost engagement and grow your following. You can ask followers to tag friends, like a post, or share your content for a chance to win a prize.
   - **Example**: A shoe store might run a giveaway where participants can enter by following the store's page and tagging two friends in the comments.
6. **Monitor Your Performance**
   - Most social media platforms provide tools to track how well your posts are performing. Keep an eye on things like likes, comments, shares, and clicks to see what types of content are resonating with your audience.

- **Example**: If a skincare brand sees that their video tutorials are getting more engagement than their photos, they might decide to create more video content.

Paid Social Media Advertising

In addition to organic (free) posts, businesses can also use paid advertising on social media to reach a larger audience. Paid social media ads allow you to promote your content to specific groups of people based on their interests, age, location, and more.

1. **Boosted Posts**
    - A boosted post is a regular post that you pay to show to a larger audience. This helps your post reach people beyond your followers, increasing visibility and engagement.
    - **Example**: A fitness brand might boost a post about a new line of workout gear to reach more fitness enthusiasts.
2. **Sponsored Ads**
    - Sponsored ads are custom-designed ads that appear in people's feeds, even if they don't follow your page. These ads can include images, videos, or carousels of products and usually have a clear call-to-action like "Shop Now" or "Sign Up."
    - **Example**: A food delivery app might run a sponsored ad with a video showcasing how easy it is to order meals through their app, encouraging viewers to download it.

Challenges of Social Media Marketing

While social media marketing offers many benefits, it also has challenges:

1. **Staying Consistent**
    - Social media requires regular posting and engagement. If you don't stay active, your followers might lose interest, and your posts might not show up in their feeds as often.
2. **Algorithm Changes**
    - Social media platforms frequently change their algorithms, which can affect how many people see your posts. This means businesses have to stay flexible and adapt their strategies to stay visible.
3. **Competition**

- With so many businesses on social media, it can be hard to stand out from the crowd. It's important to create unique content that grabs attention and offers value to your audience.

Social media marketing is one of the most effective ways for businesses to connect with their audience, build a loyal following, and promote their products or services. By choosing the right platforms, creating engaging content, and interacting with followers, businesses can use social media to grow their brand and drive sales.

Whether you're posting daily updates, running contests, or using paid ads to reach a larger audience, social media marketing is a powerful tool that can help businesses.

Chapter 13: Content Marketing

Content marketing is a strategy that focuses on creating and sharing valuable, relevant content to attract and engage an audience. Instead of directly promoting products or services, the goal is to provide content that answers questions, solves problems, or entertains, building trust with your audience over time.

In this chapter, we will dive into what content marketing is, why it's so important, and how businesses can create effective content that drives traffic, builds relationships, and converts leads into customers.

What is Content Marketing?

Content marketing is all about creating and sharing content like blog posts, videos, infographics, and eBooks that provide value to your target audience. This content is meant to inform, entertain, or educate, while also subtly promoting your business. The key to successful content marketing is delivering the right message to the right audience in a way that feels helpful, not pushy. Unlike traditional advertising, content marketing doesn't directly sell a product. Instead, it builds trust by positioning your business as an expert in your industry. Over time, people will start to view your brand as a valuable resource, which makes them more likely to choose your product or service when they're ready to make a purchase.

Why is Content Marketing Important?

1. **Builds Trust and Authority**
   - When you consistently produce high-quality content that answers your audience's questions or solves their problems, you establish your business as a trusted expert in your industry. Over time, people come to rely on your brand for advice, which makes them more likely to become customers.
   - **Example**: A skincare brand might create blog posts about different skin types and how to care for them. By providing this helpful information, they build trust with their audience.
2. **Increases Website Traffic**
   - Every piece of content you create gives people a reason to visit your website. The more valuable content you have, the more opportunities there are for people to find your business online.

- **Example**: A fitness trainer might create a YouTube channel filled with workout videos. People looking for workout routines will find the videos, leading them to visit the trainer's website.

3. **Generates Leads**
    - Content marketing can be used to generate leads by offering something valuable in exchange for a visitor's contact information, like an eBook or a free guide.
    - **Example**: A digital marketing agency might offer a free downloadable guide to creating effective social media ads, but visitors need to provide their email address to access it. This helps the agency grow its email list and attract potential customers.
4. **Improves SEO**
    - Search engines like Google reward websites that regularly produce valuable content by ranking them higher in search results. When your website ranks higher, more people find your business.
    - **Example**: A bakery that publishes blog posts about different types of bread-making techniques is more likely to show up in Google search results when someone looks up "how to bake bread."
5. **Engages Your Audience**
    - Content marketing allows you to engage your audience through comments, social media shares, and other interactions. This helps build a stronger connection between your business and your customers.
    - **Example**: A tech company might post a video tutorial on how to use their latest software and invite viewers to leave questions in the comments. This sparks conversation and keeps the audience engaged.

Types of Content Marketing

There are many different types of content marketing, each serving a unique purpose. Here are some of the most common types of content businesses use to engage their audience:

1. **Blog Posts**

- Blogging is one of the most popular forms of content marketing. Regularly publishing blog posts helps drive traffic to your website and establishes your business as an authority in your industry.
- **Example**: A travel agency might blog about different vacation destinations, offering tips on the best times to visit and must-see attractions.

2. **Videos**
   - Video content is highly engaging and often more memorable than text-based content. Whether you're creating tutorials, product demos, or behind-the-scenes videos, this type of content can help bring your brand to life.
   - **Example**: A car dealership might create video tours of new cars, showing off their features and performance to potential buyers.
3. **Infographics**
   - Infographics are visual representations of information. They are great for breaking down complex topics in a way that's easy to understand.
   - **Example**: A nutritionist might create an infographic showing the benefits of different vitamins and minerals, making it easier for people to understand the value of a balanced diet.
4. **eBooks and White Papers**
   - eBooks and white papers are more in-depth than blog posts and are usually offered as a downloadable resource in exchange for contact information. These longer-form content pieces are great for educating your audience about a specific topic.
   - **Example**: A software company might offer a white paper that explains the latest trends in cybersecurity and how businesses can protect their data.
5. **Podcasts**
   - Podcasts allow businesses to connect with their audience in a more casual, conversational format. They are great for sharing insights, interviews, and stories that align with your brand's message.
   - **Example**: A personal finance advisor might host a weekly podcast offering tips on budgeting, investing, and managing money.

How to Create a Content Marketing Strategy

To get the most out of content marketing, it's important to have a clear strategy. Here are some steps to help you create an effective content marketing plan:

1. **Know Your Audience**
    - Before creating any content, it's essential to understand who your target audience is. What are their pain points? What problems are they trying to solve? Once you know this, you can create content that speaks directly to their needs.
    - **Example**: A company selling eco-friendly products might target environmentally-conscious consumers who want to reduce their carbon footprint.
2. **Set Clear Goals**
    - Decide what you want to achieve with your content marketing efforts. Are you trying to drive traffic to your website, generate leads, or boost brand awareness? Your goals will help guide the type of content you create.
    - **Example**: A local restaurant might set a goal of increasing foot traffic by promoting their new menu through blog posts and social media.
3. **Create a Content Calendar**
    - Consistency is key to successful content marketing. Plan out your content in advance by creating a calendar that outlines what you'll publish and when.
    - **Example**: A fitness coach might plan to post a new workout video every Monday and a blog post with healthy recipes every Wednesday.
4. **Distribute Your Content**
    - Creating content is just one part of the process. You also need to promote it! Share your content on social media, in emails, and across other platforms to reach as many people as possible.
    - **Example**: After publishing a blog post, an online retailer might share it on Facebook, Instagram, and Pinterest to drive traffic back to their website.
5. **Measure Your Success**
    - Track how well your content is performing by looking at metrics like website traffic, social shares, and leads generated. Use this information to improve your strategy and create even better content in the future.

- **Example**: A nonprofit organization might measure the success of their content by how many new email subscribers they gain after releasing a series of informational blog posts.

Challenges of Content Marketing

While content marketing can be highly effective, it's not without its challenges:

1. **Time-Consuming**
   - Creating high-quality content takes time. From brainstorming ideas to writing, editing, and promoting, content marketing requires a significant investment of time and resources.
2. **Competition**
   - With so much content being published online, it can be difficult to stand out. It's important to create unique, valuable content that sets your business apart from competitors.
3. **Measuring ROI**
   - Measuring the return on investment (ROI) of content marketing can be tricky, especially since it's often a long-term strategy. However, tracking metrics like website traffic, leads, and sales can help you understand how well your content is performing.

Content marketing is a powerful tool for businesses looking to build trust, engage their audience, and drive sales. By creating valuable content that speaks to your audience's needs, you can position your business as a leader in your industry and keep customers coming back for more. Whether it's through blog posts, videos, or infographics, the key to success is providing content that's helpful, interesting, and relevant.

Chapter 14: Affiliate Marketing

Affiliate marketing is a strategy where businesses partner with other individuals or companies (called affiliates) to promote their products or services. These affiliates earn a commission for every sale, click, or action that they drive to the business through their marketing efforts. It's a win-win strategy where businesses can expand their reach without having to do all the marketing themselves, and affiliates can earn money by promoting products they believe in.

In this chapter, we will explore how affiliate marketing works, why it's an effective strategy, and how businesses can create successful affiliate programs.

What is Affiliate Marketing?

Affiliate marketing is a type of performance-based marketing where businesses reward affiliates for driving traffic or sales. Affiliates use their own platforms—like blogs, social media, or websites—to promote a business's products. When someone clicks on the affiliate's link and makes a purchase or completes a specific action, the affiliate earns a commission.

It's important to note that affiliate marketing isn't about pushing sales in an aggressive way. The best affiliate marketers provide useful content or reviews that genuinely help their audience make informed decisions.

How Affiliate Marketing Works

The process of affiliate marketing involves three main players:

1. **The Business (Merchant)**
    - This is the company that sells the product or service. They create an affiliate program and offer commissions to people (affiliates) who promote their products.
2. **The Affiliate**
    - Affiliates are the individuals or companies that promote the merchant's products. They do this by sharing links, banners, or other content that directs their audience to the merchant's site. When someone buys a product through the affiliate's link, the affiliate earns a commission.
3. **The Customer**

- The customer is the person who clicks on the affiliate's link and makes a purchase or takes another action, like signing up for a newsletter.

4. The process usually looks like this:
5. The affiliate signs up for the business's affiliate program.
6. The affiliate gets a unique link to promote the product.
7. The affiliate shares the link on their website, blog, social media, or other channels.
8. When someone clicks the link and completes a purchase, the affiliate earns a commission.

Why Affiliate Marketing is Effective

1. **Low-Risk for Businesses**
    - One of the best things about affiliate marketing is that businesses only pay for results. Since affiliates only get paid when they drive a sale or action, there's little risk of spending money on marketing that doesn't work.
2. **Expands Your Reach**
    - By partnering with affiliates, businesses can tap into new audiences that they might not have been able to reach on their own. Affiliates often have loyal followers who trust their recommendations, which can lead to more sales.
3. **Boosts Credibility**
    - When a trusted affiliate recommends a product, it adds credibility. People are more likely to buy a product when someone they trust says it's good.
4. **Scalable**
    - Affiliate marketing is scalable because businesses can work with an unlimited number of affiliates. As more affiliates join the program and promote the products, businesses can see exponential growth in sales.

Creating a Successful Affiliate Program

To create a successful affiliate marketing program, businesses need to plan and structure the program carefully. Here are the steps to get started:

1. **Set Clear Goals**

- Before starting an affiliate program, businesses need to determine what they want to achieve. Are they looking to drive more sales, increase brand awareness, or attract new customers? Setting clear goals will help define the structure of the program.

2. **Choose the Right Affiliates**
   - Not every affiliate will be the right fit for every business. It's important to find affiliates who align with the company's brand and audience. For example, a fitness brand would want to partner with influencers, bloggers, or websites that focus on health, wellness, and fitness.
3. **Offer Competitive Commissions**
   - To attract high-quality affiliates, businesses need to offer competitive commission rates. This could be a percentage of sales or a fixed fee for certain actions. For example, an online store might offer affiliates 10-20% commission on each sale.
4. **Provide Marketing Tools**
   - Successful affiliate programs provide affiliates with the tools they need to promote the products effectively. This could include banners, product images, promotional videos, and email templates.
5. **Track Performance**
   - It's important to track how well affiliates are performing. Many affiliate programs use tracking software that monitors clicks, conversions, and commissions in real-time. This helps businesses identify their top-performing affiliates and optimize the program.
6. **Build Strong Relationships**
   - Maintaining a good relationship with affiliates is key to a successful program. Businesses should keep affiliates informed about new products, sales, and promotions. Offering exclusive deals or bonuses can also help motivate affiliates to promote the products more.

Tips for Affiliates

For those who want to become affiliates, here are some tips for success:

1. **Choose Products You Believe In**

- Successful affiliate marketers promote products they genuinely believe in. When you are passionate about a product, it shows in your content, and your audience is more likely to trust your recommendation.

2. **Provide Value**
   - Instead of just placing a bunch of ads on your site, focus on providing value to your audience. Write product reviews, create how-to guides, or share personal experiences with the product. This builds trust and increases the chances of conversions.
3. **Be Transparent**
   - Always disclose that you are using affiliate links. Most countries have regulations that require affiliates to disclose when they are getting paid for promoting a product. Being transparent builds trust with your audience and helps you avoid legal issues.
4. **Track Your Performance**
   - Use tracking tools to monitor which affiliate links are performing the best. This helps you understand what's working and what isn't, so you can adjust your strategy.

Challenges of Affiliate Marketing

While affiliate marketing can be highly effective, it does come with some challenges:

1. **Finding the Right Affiliates**
   - Not all affiliates will perform well. Some may not have the right audience or may not be as dedicated to promoting the products. It can take time to find the right affiliates who are a good fit for your brand.
2. **Competition**
   - Depending on the industry, affiliate marketing can be highly competitive. Affiliates often promote similar products, so businesses need to stand out by offering competitive commissions and unique selling points.
3. **Monitoring Fraud**
   - There is always a risk of fraudulent activity in affiliate marketing, such as affiliates generating fake traffic or clicks to earn commissions. Businesses need to have systems in place to detect and prevent fraud.

Affiliate marketing is a powerful and cost-effective way for businesses to grow their sales and reach new audiences. By partnering with affiliates, businesses can tap into the influence and credibility of others, driving more traffic and conversions. Whether you're a business looking to create an affiliate program or an individual interested in becoming an affiliate, success in affiliate marketing comes from building strong relationships, providing value, and tracking performance.
Affiliate marketing allows businesses to grow in a sustainable and scalable way, all while rewarding affiliates for their efforts.

Part 4: Advanced Marketing Techniques

Chapter 15: Benefits of Effective Marketing

Marketing is the bridge between a business and its customers. It helps businesses connect with their audience, promote products or services, and ultimately drive sales. Effective marketing goes beyond just telling people about your products; it helps build a brand, engage with customers, and create lasting relationships that benefit both the business and the customer.
In this chapter, we'll explore the key benefits of effective marketing, including how it can shape a brand, engage your audience, and increase sales.

---

1. Building a Strong Brand

A brand is more than just a logo or a name—it's the identity of a business, including its values, mission, and how it is perceived by the public. Marketing plays a critical role in shaping and maintaining a brand.

- **Brand Recognition**: Effective marketing helps people recognize your brand and understand what it stands for. Consistent marketing messages across different platforms (like social media, websites, and ads) reinforce your brand identity.
- **Differentiation**: Marketing can highlight what makes your brand unique. By promoting the features or values that set your business apart from competitors, marketing helps customers understand why they should choose your product or service over others.
- **Building Trust**: Regularly engaging with your audience through valuable content and customer service builds trust over time. Trust is essential for customer loyalty, as people are more likely to return to a brand they trust.

---

2. Engaging with Your Audience

Customer engagement is about more than just making a sale. It's about creating a relationship between the business and the customer, where they feel valued and heard. Marketing provides the tools to engage with your audience in meaningful ways.

- **Two-Way Communication**: With modern marketing channels like social media, businesses can have direct conversations with their customers. Customers can comment on posts, ask questions, or share feedback, and businesses can respond in real-time, making the customer feel valued.
- **Personalization**: Marketing allows businesses to personalize their messages based on customer data, making the customer feel like the brand understands their individual needs. For example, sending personalized emails with product recommendations based on past purchases shows customers that their preferences matter.
- **Creating Communities**: Some brands use marketing to build communities around their products or services. This can be done through online forums, social media groups, or hosting events. A strong community can turn customers into loyal advocates who help promote the brand to others.

---

3. Driving Sales and Business Growth

At the end of the day, the primary goal of marketing is to increase sales and grow the business. Effective marketing helps drive this growth in several ways:

- **Attracting New Customers**: Marketing spreads the word about your products or services, helping you reach new audiences. Whether it's through advertisements, social media, or content marketing, a well-executed strategy can bring in new customers who may not have heard of your business otherwise.
- **Increasing Conversion Rates**: Marketing isn't just about getting people to visit your website or store; it's about convincing them to make a purchase. Through tactics like email campaigns, promotions, and personalized recommendations, businesses can guide potential customers toward making a buying decision.

- **Encouraging Repeat Business**: It's more cost-effective to keep existing customers than to find new ones, and marketing helps businesses stay in touch with their customers. Loyalty programs, special offers, and consistent communication can encourage customers to return and make additional purchases.

---

4. Measuring Success and Improving Over Time

One of the great things about modern marketing is that it's measurable. With the right tools, businesses can track how well their marketing campaigns are performing and make adjustments to improve results.

- **Data-Driven Decisions**: Marketing platforms provide businesses with data on customer behavior, such as which ads are getting clicks or what products are most popular. This information helps businesses understand what's working and what isn't, allowing them to tweak their strategy for better results.
- **Continuous Improvement**: Effective marketing is never a one-time effort. It's an ongoing process that requires regular updates and improvements. By measuring performance and staying flexible, businesses can keep their marketing strategies fresh and effective.

Effective marketing is essential for any business that wants to succeed in today's competitive environment. It helps businesses build a strong brand, engage with their audience, drive sales, and continuously improve their strategies. Whether you're a small start-up or a large corporation, investing in marketing is key to long-term growth and success.

Chapter 16: Identifying Market Saturation Risks

In the world of business, market saturation occurs when a product or service has been widely distributed and consumed, leaving little room for new competitors to enter the market or existing businesses to grow. This chapter will explain how businesses can recognize the risks of market saturation, how it can impact them, and strategies to stand out in a crowded market.

What is Market Saturation?

Market saturation happens when a product or service has reached maximum potential within a market. This means that most consumers who are interested in that product or service already own it or have access to it, making it difficult for businesses to find new customers.

For example, imagine there are many smartphone companies, and most people already have a phone. It becomes challenging for any new company to convince people to buy their new phone unless they offer something significantly different.

The Risks of Market Saturation

1. **Decreased Growth**
    - When a market is saturated, businesses may find it hard to grow. There are fewer new customers to attract, and existing customers might not need to buy replacements for a long time. This slows down the growth of the company.
2. **Increased Competition**
    - In a saturated market, competition can become fierce. Businesses may start offering discounts or promotions to attract customers, leading to a price war. This reduces profit margins and can hurt smaller companies that can't afford to compete on price.
3. **Customer Fatigue**
    - Customers may become overwhelmed or uninterested in a product that is too widely available. When every business offers similar products, it's harder to stand out, and customers may lose interest altogether.

How to Recognize Market Saturation

Businesses can recognize the signs of market saturation by keeping an eye on several factors:

1. **Stagnant Sales Growth**
    - If sales growth starts to slow down, despite strong marketing efforts, it could be a sign that the market is becoming saturated. This suggests that there may be fewer new customers to attract.
2. **Increased Competitor Activity**
    - When many competitors enter the market offering similar products or services, it's a signal that the market may be approaching saturation. This is especially true if companies start competing aggressively on price or promotions.
3. **Fewer Repeat Customers**
    - In a saturated market, customers may stop returning for repeat purchases because they either have what they need or there are too many other options available.

Strategies to Overcome Market Saturation

Even in a saturated market, businesses can still find ways to thrive by differentiating themselves and offering unique value. Here are some strategies to help businesses stand out:

1. **Innovate**
    - One of the best ways to combat market saturation is through innovation. Businesses can create new features, improve existing products, or introduce entirely new services to attract attention. By offering something different, businesses can set themselves apart from the competition.
    - **Example**: A tech company might introduce a new feature on its smartphone that makes it more desirable than existing phones, like a long-lasting battery or better camera quality.
2. **Target Niche Markets**
    - Instead of trying to compete with everyone, businesses can focus on a smaller, more specific audience. By catering to the needs of a niche market, companies can create loyal customers who feel that their unique needs are being addressed.

- **Example**: A clothing brand might start targeting eco-conscious consumers by creating a line of environmentally friendly clothing.

3. **Improve Customer Experience**
    - In a saturated market, the customer experience can be a major differentiator. Businesses that go above and beyond to provide excellent customer service, personalized experiences, and added value can build stronger relationships with their customers and stand out.
    - **Example**: A restaurant might offer personalized service, such as remembering customers' preferences or offering special discounts to loyal customers.
4. **Diversify Product Offerings**
    - Another way to survive market saturation is by diversifying product lines. Expanding the range of products or services offered can open up new revenue streams and attract a different customer base.
    - **Example**: A coffee shop could start offering baked goods or sandwiches, not just coffee, to attract customers who may not be primarily looking for coffee.
5. **Focus on Brand Loyalty**
    - Building strong relationships with existing customers can help businesses maintain their market share even in a saturated environment. Loyalty programs, exclusive offers, and personalized marketing can keep customers coming back, even when there are many other options available.
    - **Example**: A fitness brand could offer rewards points for repeat customers that can be redeemed for discounts on future purchases.

Market saturation presents challenges for businesses trying to grow in a highly competitive environment. However, by recognizing the signs of saturation and implementing strategies like innovation, targeting niche markets, and improving customer experience, businesses can continue to thrive even in crowded markets. By standing out from the competition and staying connected with loyal customers, businesses can maintain success and find new opportunities for growth.

Chapter 17: Addressing Devaluation and Customer Bias

In the world of marketing and business operations, one of the challenges businesses face is the risk of devaluation and dealing with customer bias. Devaluation occurs when customers begin to perceive your product or service as less valuable, and this perception can harm your brand's reputation, reducing sales and customer loyalty. Bias, on the other hand, involves customers forming preconceived notions about your product, often based on stereotypes or past experiences, which can also affect their purchasing decisions.
In this chapter, we'll explore strategies to maintain product value, overcome customer bias, and ensure that your business continues to thrive despite these challenges.

What is Devaluation?

Devaluation happens when customers start to believe that a product is not worth its price. This perception may arise because of various factors, including increased competition, poor marketing, or even external economic factors. When a product is seen as devalued, people may stop buying it or only consider it if the price is drastically reduced.

Factors that Lead to Devaluation

1. **Oversupply in the Market**
    - When there are too many similar products on the market, your product may lose its uniqueness. For example, if too many competitors are selling nearly identical items, customers may no longer see why they should choose yours.
2. **Price Wars**
    - When companies continuously lower their prices to outdo their competitors, it can make customers believe that the product is only valuable at a lower price, leading to an overall devaluation of the product or service.
3. **Stale Marketing**
    - If your marketing strategies do not evolve, your brand might seem outdated or unappealing. Customers are attracted to new and exciting experiences, and a brand that doesn't refresh its image might lose relevance in the eyes of its target audience.

4. **Negative Reviews or Poor Customer Experiences**
   - Word-of-mouth and online reviews play a huge role in shaping customer perception. A series of negative reviews or a viral incident of poor customer service can quickly damage your brand's value in the eyes of the public.

What is Customer Bias?

Customer bias refers to the preconceived notions that consumers have about a product or brand before even experiencing it. This bias can be either positive or negative and often stems from cultural influences, personal experiences, or external recommendations.

- **Example**: A customer might avoid buying a product from a certain company because they've had a bad experience with the brand before, or they might favor a brand simply because it's the most popular, even if it's not necessarily the best.

Types of Customer Bias

1. **Price Bias**
   - Some customers believe that a higher price automatically means a better product, while others assume that lower-priced items offer better value for money.
2. **Brand Loyalty Bias**
   - Customers who have a strong loyalty to a particular brand might ignore other alternatives, even if those alternatives offer better features or value.
3. **Cultural or Societal Bias**
   - Certain products may be viewed more positively or negatively based on cultural trends or societal values. For instance, eco-friendly products tend to be favored in today's environmentally conscious market, while fast-fashion brands may face backlash for their environmental impact.

Strategies to Prevent Devaluation and Overcome Customer Bias

1. **Deliver Consistent Quality**

- One of the most important ways to maintain your product's value is by ensuring consistent quality. If customers know they can rely on your brand for a high-quality product every time, they are less likely to perceive it as devalued, even if there's competition or economic shifts.
- **Example**: A premium shoe brand that always uses top-quality materials can justify its higher price and maintain its reputation despite lower-cost alternatives.

2. **Build a Strong Brand Image**
    - Building a strong and consistent brand image helps keep your product from being devalued. Your brand should tell a story that resonates with your target audience, showcasing what makes your product unique and valuable.
    - **Example**: Apple maintains its brand image of innovation, luxury, and sleek design, which allows it to price its products higher than many competitors.
3. **Innovate Regularly**
    - To stay competitive and keep your brand from being devalued, innovation is key. Whether it's through new product features, better customer service, or updated marketing strategies, businesses must continuously evolve to stay relevant.
    - **Example**: A tech company that regularly releases updates and new features for its products is more likely to retain customer interest and maintain product value.
4. **Engage with Customers**
    - Customer engagement is crucial for overcoming bias. By responding to customer feedback, addressing concerns, and providing personalized experiences, businesses can shift negative perceptions and foster a more positive relationship with their audience.
    - **Example**: A restaurant chain that receives a bad review might offer the customer a free meal or special offer to improve their experience and potentially win back their trust.
5. **Educate Your Audience**
    - Sometimes, customers simply don't understand why your product is worth its price or how it stands out from competitors. Through informative content, such as blog posts, videos, or even live demonstrations, businesses can educate their audience and overcome biases rooted in misunderstanding.

- **Example**: A cosmetics brand might create tutorials showing how to use their products and highlight why their ingredients are more effective than cheaper alternatives.

6. **Leverage Positive Reviews and Testimonials**
   - Positive reviews and testimonials from happy customers can be powerful tools for combating bias and maintaining value. Featuring real customer stories or reviews on your website, social media, and advertisements can help sway hesitant buyers.
   - **Example**: A clothing brand may share photos and testimonials from influencers or regular customers who love their products, providing social proof that helps convince new customers.

Devaluation and customer bias are challenges that all businesses face at some point, but with the right strategies, these challenges can be overcome. By focusing on consistent quality, innovation, customer engagement, and education, businesses can protect their brand's value and create a positive, lasting impression with their audience.

Chapter 18: Marketing During Economic Downturns

When the economy hits a rough patch, businesses can face significant challenges. Customers spend less money, and competition for the limited spending power becomes fierce. However, marketing during economic downturns is not about giving up; it's about adjusting strategies to fit the changing landscape. This chapter will discuss the importance of maintaining marketing efforts during tough economic times, how to adjust your approach, and key strategies to survive and even thrive during these periods.

Why Marketing is Still Important During a Downturn

1. **Maintaining Visibility**
   - In an economic downturn, many businesses make the mistake of cutting their marketing budgets. While this can save money in the short term, it makes the brand less visible when consumers are already being more selective with their spending. If a business reduces its marketing presence, customers may forget about the brand, leading to a drop in sales.
2. **Building Trust and Stability**
   - Consumers want to feel reassured during uncertain times. Brands that stay visible and communicate consistently during a downturn are seen as stable and reliable. This builds trust with customers, which can lead to long-term loyalty.
   - **Example**: A grocery chain might emphasize that they're working hard to keep shelves stocked and prices fair, providing a sense of security to their customers.
3. **Taking Advantage of Less Competition**
   - When other businesses cut back on their marketing, the field becomes less crowded. This creates an opportunity for businesses that continue marketing efforts to stand out more and gain market share.
   - **Example**: A local restaurant might increase its online advertising when competitors are cutting back, gaining more attention from people looking for dining options.

How to Adjust Marketing Strategies During a Downturn

1. **Focus on Value**
   - During a recession, consumers are more careful with their spending. Marketing should focus on the value your product or service offers. This doesn't always mean lowering prices, but rather highlighting how your product solves problems or improves life at a reasonable cost.
   - **Example**: A phone company might highlight how their affordable service plans help customers save money without sacrificing quality.
2. **Shift to Digital Channels**
   - Digital marketing is often more cost-effective than traditional advertising methods like TV or print. During an economic downturn, shifting your focus to social media, email marketing, and content marketing can help you maintain visibility without overspending.
   - **Example**: A fitness brand might create home workout videos and share them on social media to engage customers who are looking for affordable fitness solutions.
3. **Nurture Existing Customers**
   - It's more expensive to acquire new customers than to keep existing ones. During tough economic times, businesses should focus on retaining their current customers by offering excellent service, personalized experiences, and loyalty rewards.
   - **Example**: A beauty brand might offer discounts to loyal customers or create a rewards program that gives them special perks for repeat purchases.
4. **Adapt Your Messaging**
   - Marketing messages should reflect the current reality that customers are facing. Instead of using flashy or extravagant marketing, focus on empathy, understanding, and support. Show that your business understands the challenges people are going through and is there to help.
   - **Example**: A bank might offer financial advice through blog posts or webinars, helping customers manage their money better during tough times.

Marketing Strategies to Thrive During a Recession

1. **Offer Flexible Payment Options**
   - Many people experience financial strain during a downturn, so offering flexible payment options can make your products more accessible. This could include installment payments, financing, or subscription models.
   - **Example**: A tech company might allow customers to pay for a new computer in smaller monthly installments, making it easier to afford during tough financial times.
2. **Prioritize Customer Feedback**
   - Listening to customer feedback becomes even more critical during economic downturns. Customers' needs and priorities may shift, and businesses that respond to these changes are more likely to succeed.
   - **Example**: A food delivery service might survey customers to find out what promotions or new services would help them most during the recession, then adapt their offerings accordingly.
3. **Strengthen Your Online Presence**
   - With more people spending time online, businesses should ensure that their websites and social media platforms are up-to-date and easy to use. Offering online shopping, live chat customer service, and easy-to-navigate websites can help drive sales during a downturn.
   - **Example**: A clothing retailer could enhance its website with features like virtual try-ons or live chat support to help hesitant shoppers make purchase decisions.
4. **Collaborate with Other Businesses**
   - Collaboration can help businesses expand their reach and offer more value to customers. Partnering with complementary businesses allows you to pool resources, share audiences, and create joint promotions that benefit both brands.
   - **Example**: A coffee shop might partner with a local bakery to create a special "coffee and pastry" promotion, driving traffic to both businesses.

Marketing during an economic downturn requires adaptability and a clear understanding of your customers' needs. By focusing on value, maintaining a strong online presence, and offering flexible options, businesses can not only survive but also find new opportunities for growth. A downturn doesn't mean marketing should stop—it just means marketing needs to be smarter and more in tune with the changing economic landscape.

Part 5: Building a Marketing Funnel

Chapter 19: The Awareness Stage

In the marketing world, creating awareness for your product or service is the first critical step in a marketing funnel. The awareness stage is all about introducing your brand to potential customers who might not have known about it before. At this point, you are not trying to make a hard sell but rather building a foundation of trust and familiarity.

This chapter will explain what the awareness stage is, why it's important, and strategies businesses can use to successfully get their brand in front of their target audience.

What is the Awareness Stage?

The awareness stage is the very top of the marketing funnel. It's where potential customers first come across your business, but they're not necessarily ready to buy yet. At this stage, they might just be identifying a need or problem and are exploring options to address it. Your goal is to make sure they know your brand exists and can solve their problem.

Think of this stage as laying the groundwork. If customers don't know about your business, they won't consider you when they're ready to make a purchase. That's why awareness is so important.

Why is the Awareness Stage Important?

1. **Brand Visibility**
    - For customers to even consider buying from you, they first need to know you exist. The awareness stage helps your business become visible to people who have never heard of you before. Without awareness, even the best products or services may go unnoticed.
2. **Building Trust**

   - People are more likely to buy from businesses they recognize and trust. The awareness stage is your chance to start building that trust. When potential customers see your brand consistently, they begin to feel more comfortable with it.
3. **Setting the Foundation**
   - The awareness stage sets the foundation for future engagement. You're not pushing for a sale yet—you're just introducing your brand and showing potential customers that you can help solve their problems.

How to Create Awareness

There are many ways to create awareness for your business, and the best strategies often depend on your industry and target audience. Here are some of the most effective ways to build awareness:

1. **Content Marketing**
   - Content marketing involves creating valuable, informative content that your target audience finds helpful. This content can be in the form of blog posts, videos, infographics, or social media posts. The goal is to provide useful information that introduces your brand as an expert in your field.
   - **Example**: A fitness trainer could create blog posts or YouTube videos about healthy living tips, exercise routines, or nutrition advice. These pieces of content would help potential clients become aware of the trainer and start building trust in their expertise.
2. **Social Media**
   - Social media platforms like Instagram, TikTok, and Twitter offer great opportunities to introduce your brand to a wider audience. By creating engaging posts and using relevant hashtags, you can reach potential customers who may not have known about your business.
   - **Example**: A small business selling eco-friendly clothing could use Instagram to post pictures of their products, along with stories about the materials they use. This content could reach users who are interested in sustainability and looking for brands that align with their values.
3. **Search Engine Optimization (SEO)**

- SEO involves optimizing your website and content so that it ranks higher on search engine results pages (like Google). When people search for something related to your business, your website should appear at the top of the search results. This is a key way to attract potential customers who are looking for solutions to their problems.
- **Example**: A local bakery might optimize its website for the keyword "best cupcakes in [city name]." When someone searches for this phrase, the bakery's website could appear in the top search results, helping them attract new customers.

4. **Paid Advertising**
   - Paid advertising, such as Google Ads or social media ads, can help you get in front of people who are likely interested in your products or services. You can target specific demographics, interests, or search terms to make sure your ads are seen by the right audience.
   - **Example**: A new online course for learning graphic design could run ads on Facebook targeting people who have shown interest in art or design. These ads would introduce the course to people who may want to learn graphic design but haven't yet found the right program.
5. **Collaborations and Influencer Marketing**
   - Partnering with influencers or other businesses can help introduce your brand to new audiences. Influencers have loyal followers who trust their recommendations, making them a great way to create awareness for your brand.
   - **Example**: A skincare brand might partner with a beauty influencer on YouTube. The influencer could try out the products and share their experience with their followers, helping the skincare brand reach a new audience.

Best Practices for the Awareness Stage

To make the most of the awareness stage, here are a few tips to keep in mind:

1. **Know Your Audience**
   - Before you start creating content or running ads, make sure you understand who your target audience is. Knowing their demographics, interests, and pain points will help you create more effective awareness campaigns.

- **Example**: If you sell athletic gear, your target audience might include young adults who are into sports or fitness. Understanding this helps you create content that resonates with them, like workout tutorials or product demonstrations.

2. **Consistency is Key**
   - Building awareness takes time, and consistency is important. Regularly posting on social media, updating your blog, and running ads ensures that potential customers see your brand multiple times. The more they see you, the more likely they are to remember you when they're ready to buy.
3. **Track Your Performance**
   - Use analytics tools to track how well your awareness efforts are performing. For example, if you're running ads, check how many people are clicking on them. If you're posting on social media, see how many likes, shares, or comments your posts are getting. This data can help you refine your strategy and improve your results.

The awareness stage is all about making your brand visible to potential customers and laying the groundwork for future engagement. Through strategies like content marketing, social media, SEO, paid advertising, and collaborations, you can introduce your brand to the right audience and start building trust. By being consistent and tracking your performance, you can maximize the effectiveness of your awareness campaigns and set your business up for success in the next stages of the marketing funnel.

Chapter 20: Generating Interest

After you've introduced your product or service in the awareness stage, the next important step in the marketing funnel is generating interest. This stage is crucial because it moves potential customers from simply knowing about your brand to becoming more engaged and curious about what you have to offer. During this stage, businesses need to provide valuable, engaging content and offers that help nurture leads and keep them interested.

In this chapter, we will explore how to effectively generate interest, keep your audience engaged, and ensure that potential customers continue moving down the funnel toward making a purchase.

What is the Interest Stage?

The interest stage is where potential customers start to engage more deeply with your brand. At this point, they're likely asking themselves questions like:

- "How can this product solve my problem?"
- "Why should I choose this brand over others?"

Your goal in this stage is to provide answers to these questions, establish a connection with the audience, and offer valuable content that keeps them engaged. If done right, you'll create a relationship with your potential customers that moves them closer to making a purchase.

How to Generate Interest

1. **Provide Valuable Content**
    - Content marketing plays a huge role in the interest stage. You want to create content that is both informative and engaging, addressing the needs and pain points of your audience. Types of content that can generate interest include:
        - Blog posts
        - How-to videos
        - E-books or whitepapers
        - Webinars
    - **Example**: A skincare brand might create blog posts about different skin types and how to choose the best skincare routine for each. This content would help potential customers understand their own needs and see the brand as an expert in skincare solutions.

2. **Offer Lead Magnets**
    - A lead magnet is something valuable you offer to potential customers in exchange for their contact information, such as their email address. Lead magnets often come in the form of free guides, checklists, or templates. By providing valuable resources, you can keep potential customers engaged and build trust with them.
    - **Example**: A financial consulting firm might offer a free budgeting template for download. In return, they get the customer's email, allowing them to continue marketing to this lead through email campaigns.
3. **Leverage Email Marketing**
    - Once you've gathered contact information from potential customers, email marketing is a highly effective way to keep them interested. Through email newsletters, personalized offers, and updates, you can stay top-of-mind and provide additional value. Remember to avoid hard sales tactics here—focus on educating and building trust.
    - **Example**: A clothing brand might send an email with style tips or new collection updates, subtly encouraging recipients to explore their website.
4. **Use Social Media Engagement**
    - Social media is a powerful tool for keeping potential customers engaged. Through regular posts, polls, Q&A sessions, and live videos, you can create an interactive experience that encourages people to stay connected with your brand. Social platforms like Instagram, Twitter, and Facebook allow businesses to have a direct conversation with their audience.
    - **Example**: A gym might use Instagram Stories to post quick workout tips or host live Q&A sessions where followers can ask questions about fitness routines.
5. **Create Case Studies or Success Stories**
    - Sharing case studies or customer success stories helps demonstrate the real-world value of your product or service. These stories show potential customers how your offerings have positively impacted others, which can generate interest by making your solution seem relatable and effective.
    - **Example**: A software company could showcase a success story where a small business used their software to streamline operations and increase profits.

Best Practices for Generating Interest

1. **Tailor Content to Your Audience's Needs**
    - The content and offers you provide during this stage need to be relevant to your audience's specific needs. Personalization is key. The more your content speaks directly to the challenges or desires of your potential customers, the more likely they are to stay engaged.
2. **Maintain Consistent Communication**
    - You want to maintain a steady flow of communication with your audience. Whether through social media, emails, or website content, regular touchpoints help keep your brand top of mind. However, avoid overwhelming them with too much content at once—find a balance that keeps them interested without feeling bombarded.
3. **Focus on Building Relationships**
    - The goal during the interest stage isn't just to sell but to build a relationship. Show your potential customers that your brand is helpful, trustworthy, and aligned with their values. This relationship-building will make them more likely to consider your product or service when they're ready to make a purchase.
4. **Monitor Engagement Metrics**
    - It's important to track how well your interest-generating efforts are performing. Monitor engagement metrics like open rates, click-through rates, social media interactions, and website visits. This data will help you refine your strategies and improve the effectiveness of your content.

Generating interest is all about keeping potential customers engaged and nurturing them as they learn more about your brand. Through valuable content, lead magnets, email marketing, and social media engagement, businesses can create meaningful connections with their audience. By focusing on relationship-building rather than immediate sales, you can lead potential customers closer to making a purchase decision in the next stage of the funnel.

Chapter 21: Evaluation and Decision Stages

Once potential customers are aware of your product and show interest, the next steps in the marketing funnel are the **evaluation** and **decision** stages. In these stages, customers actively assess your product or service, comparing it with other options. Their goal is to decide whether your product is the best choice for them. During this process, your job is to provide all the necessary information, build trust, and give them confidence that your product is the best solution to their needs.

What Happens in the Evaluation Stage?

The evaluation stage is where potential customers are researching and weighing their options. They have already shown interest in your brand, but they aren't ready to buy just yet. Instead, they are:

- Comparing prices
- Reading reviews and testimonials
- Looking at alternatives
- Investigating features and benefits

In this phase, they want to make sure your product meets their needs and offers the best value.

How to Guide Customers in the Evaluation Stage

1. **Provide Detailed Product Information**
    - Customers want to understand everything about the product they're considering. Ensure that your website and marketing materials clearly explain the product's features, benefits, and any technical specifications. Offer comparisons between your product and similar ones to highlight what makes yours stand out.
    - **Example**: If you sell tech gadgets, create a comparison chart that shows how your product is more durable or offers better battery life than competing products.
2. **Showcase Customer Reviews and Testimonials**

- Social proof is powerful. Potential customers often rely on the experiences of others to help them make decisions. Display customer reviews and testimonials prominently on your website to reassure potential buyers that they are making the right choice.
- **Example**: An online clothing store could highlight testimonials from happy customers, sharing how the quality and fit of the clothes exceeded their expectations.

3. **Offer Case Studies or Success Stories**
    - Case studies show how your product or service has helped previous customers. These real-world examples help potential customers visualize how your product can meet their own needs.
    - **Example**: A software company might present a case study that explains how their app helped a small business streamline operations and increase productivity.
4. **Provide Free Trials or Demos**
    - Letting potential customers try your product without committing to a purchase is an effective way to move them toward a decision. Free trials, demos, or sample products allow them to experience the value firsthand, making it easier for them to choose your product.
    - **Example**: A fitness app could offer a 7-day free trial, allowing users to explore the workouts and features before deciding to subscribe.

What Happens in the Decision Stage?

In the decision stage, the customer is ready to make a purchase, but they may still need a final nudge. This is where you remove any remaining barriers to buying and make the process as easy and reassuring as possible. The goal here is to convert interest into a sale.

How to Convert Interest into a Purchase in the Decision Stage

1. **Use Clear Calls-to-Action (CTAs)**

- Make it easy for customers to take the next step. Your CTAs should be clear, visible, and action-oriented. Phrases like "Buy Now," "Sign Up Today," or "Get Started" give customers a clear path to follow.
- **Example**: An e-commerce site should have a prominent "Add to Cart" or "Buy Now" button on product pages.

2. **Offer Special Promotions or Discounts**
    - A limited-time discount or special offer can provide the final push for customers who are hesitating. Promotions like free shipping, a percentage off, or a bonus gift with purchase can make the decision easier for them.
    - **Example**: A beauty brand might offer a 10% discount to first-time buyers or throw in a free product sample for customers who make a purchase.
3. **Provide a Money-Back Guarantee**
    - A money-back guarantee reduces the perceived risk of purchasing. Customers who are unsure may feel more comfortable buying if they know they can return the product for a full refund if it doesn't meet their expectations.
    - **Example**: A company selling home fitness equipment might offer a 30-day money-back guarantee, allowing customers to return the equipment if they're not satisfied.
4. **Ensure a Smooth Checkout Process**
    - A complicated or confusing checkout process can cause customers to abandon their purchase. Make sure your checkout process is simple, fast, and secure. Avoid unnecessary steps and offer multiple payment options.
    - **Example**: An online retailer should allow guest checkouts, offer payment options like PayPal or credit cards, and minimize the number of steps needed to complete the purchase.

Building Trust in the Evaluation and Decision Stages

1. **Highlight Security and Privacy**
    - Customers want to know that their information is safe when making online purchases. Include security badges, SSL certificates, and privacy policy links to reassure customers that their data is protected.

  - **Example**: An e-commerce site might display a security badge that shows they use encrypted payment processing to protect customers' credit card information.
2. **Offer Excellent Customer Support**
  - Providing easy access to customer support can make a huge difference in helping customers make a decision. Whether it's through live chat, phone support, or email, ensure that customers can get their questions answered quickly.
  - **Example**: A software company might offer 24/7 live chat support to assist customers who are trying to decide if the product is right for them.
3. **Showcase Industry Certifications or Awards**
  - If your product or business has received any industry certifications, awards, or recognitions, make sure to highlight them. These accomplishments act as third-party endorsements and can help build trust with potential customers.
  - **Example**: A health and wellness company could display certifications showing that their products meet certain health and safety standards.

The evaluation and decision stages are crucial points in the marketing funnel. During these stages, customers are considering your product more seriously, and it's your job to provide them with all the information, reassurances, and incentives they need to make a confident decision. By offering detailed product information, customer reviews, clear CTAs, and special promotions, you can guide customers toward making a purchase and ensure that your marketing efforts lead to sales.

Chapter 22: Purchase and Post-Purchase Follow-Up

Now that potential customers have moved through the stages of awareness, interest, and decision, the next crucial step is the **purchase stage**. But the marketing journey doesn't end when someone buys your product. The **post-purchase follow-up** is just as important for creating loyal customers and encouraging repeat business.

In this chapter, we'll cover how to close the sale effectively and what businesses should do after the purchase to keep customers happy, loyal, and ready to buy again.

The Purchase Stage

The purchase stage is the moment when a customer finally decides to buy your product or service. This is the culmination of all your marketing efforts so far, but there are still some key actions to take during this phase to ensure that the buying process is smooth and satisfying.

How to Optimize the Purchase Process

1. **Provide a Seamless Checkout Experience**
    - The checkout process should be quick, easy, and intuitive. Complicated or slow checkouts can cause customers to abandon their purchase at the last minute. Make sure your payment system is secure, simple, and accessible on mobile devices.
    - **Example**: An online store should offer multiple payment options like credit cards, PayPal, or Apple Pay, allowing customers to choose their preferred method.
2. **Offer Clear Calls to Action (CTAs)**
    - Ensure that CTAs like "Buy Now" or "Proceed to Checkout" are easy to find and understand. Customers should know exactly what step to take next without feeling overwhelmed by too many choices.
    - **Example**: A clothing store website could have a clear "Add to Cart" button below each item and a "Proceed to Checkout" button that stands out.

3. **Provide Shipping and Delivery Information**
    - Customers like to know when they can expect their order, so it's important to provide accurate shipping details, estimated delivery times, and any tracking information. Offering free or fast shipping can also encourage purchases.
    - **Example**: An electronics retailer might display a countdown for "Order by 5 p.m. for next-day delivery" to create a sense of urgency.
4. **Include a Money-Back Guarantee or Return Policy**
    - A clear return policy or money-back guarantee reassures customers that they're not taking a risk by buying your product. Knowing they can return it if needed makes them more likely to complete the purchase.
    - **Example**: A skincare brand could offer a 30-day money-back guarantee for customers who aren't satisfied with their results.

The Importance of Post-Purchase Follow-Up

After a customer makes a purchase, it's essential to follow up to ensure they're satisfied and encourage them to become a repeat customer. The post-purchase phase is an opportunity to build a relationship with your customers and keep them engaged with your brand.

How to Create an Effective Post-Purchase Experience

1. **Send a Thank-You Email**
    - Sending a personalized thank-you email after a purchase is a simple way to show appreciation. This email can include the order details, delivery information, and an invitation to contact customer service if needed.
    - **Example**: An online bookstore could send an email saying, "Thank you for your purchase! Your order will be delivered in 3–5 days. If you have any questions, feel free to reach out!"
2. **Ask for Feedback or Reviews**
    - Asking customers for their feedback helps you improve your products or services and shows that you care about their experience. You can encourage customers to leave reviews or participate in surveys.

- **Example**: A home goods store might send a follow-up email asking, "How did you like your new furniture? Leave a review and let us know!"

3. **Provide Tips and Tutorials**
   - Helping customers get the most out of their purchase is a great way to keep them engaged. Providing helpful tips, tutorials, or care instructions makes the post-purchase experience positive and keeps customers connected to your brand.
   - **Example**: A fitness equipment brand could send a guide on how to use their product properly or offer workout plans to help customers achieve their fitness goals.
4. **Offer a Discount or Incentive for the Next Purchase**
   - Encouraging customers to return for another purchase is easier when you offer them an incentive. A discount on their next order or access to a special promotion makes them more likely to buy from you again.
   - **Example**: A clothing retailer might offer a 10% discount on the customer's next purchase, encouraging them to return soon.
5. **Enroll Customers in a Loyalty Program**
   - Loyalty programs reward customers for making repeat purchases and can include perks like exclusive offers, early access to new products, or discounts. These programs help build a long-term relationship with customers.
   - **Example**: A coffee shop chain could offer a points-based loyalty program where customers earn points for every purchase that can be redeemed for free drinks.

Dealing with Post-Purchase Issues

Not every purchase goes perfectly. Whether it's a delayed delivery, a faulty product, or a customer who isn't satisfied, how you handle post-purchase issues can make or break the customer relationship.

1. **Offer Fast and Friendly Customer Support**
   - Customers should be able to reach your support team easily if they have any problems. Whether through phone, email, or live chat, ensure that customer service is prompt and helpful.
   - **Example**: An electronics company could offer 24/7 customer support to help customers with setup issues or technical problems.
2. **Resolve Complaints Quickly**

- When things go wrong, resolving the issue quickly and professionally is key to keeping the customer's trust. Offering a replacement or refund without hassle shows that you value their satisfaction.
- **Example**: A shoe company might offer to replace a pair of shoes free of charge if a customer receives the wrong size.

3. **Provide Clear Return Instructions**
   - If a customer needs to return an item, make the process as easy as possible. Provide clear return instructions and offer a pre-paid shipping label if necessary.
   - **Example**: A fashion brand could include a return slip and a pre-paid label in every shipment to simplify returns.

The purchase and post-purchase follow-up stages are critical to turning one-time buyers into loyal customers. By providing a seamless checkout experience, following up with personalized communication, and offering excellent customer support, businesses can ensure that their customers feel valued and encouraged to return. These efforts build trust, boost customer satisfaction, and create opportunities for future growth.

Part 6: Revenue and Profit Optimization

Chapter 23: Multiple Revenue Streams

When running a business, relying on just one way to make money can be risky. What happens if something goes wrong, like a drop in sales or a change in customer demand? This is why having **multiple revenue streams**—different ways of making money—can help protect and grow a business. By diversifying your income, you increase your chances of long-term success and reduce the risk of your business failing if one stream dries up.

In this chapter, we'll explore why it's important to develop multiple sources of income for your business and how you can create new streams to boost profitability.

Why Multiple Revenue Streams are Important

1. **Stability During Uncertain Times**
   - If your business relies on just one source of income, any disruption—like a drop in customer interest or an economic downturn—could have a huge impact. However, if you have several streams of revenue, you can still make money even if one area of your business slows down.
   - **Example**: A local coffee shop that sells drinks might also sell branded mugs, coffee beans, and offer online subscriptions for home delivery. If fewer people visit the shop in person, online sales or subscriptions help keep the business going.
2. **Opportunities for Growth**
   - Expanding your business with different revenue streams allows you to reach new customers and explore more ways to grow. You might discover untapped markets that are interested in what you offer.
   - **Example**: An artist who typically sells paintings in a gallery might start selling digital art prints online, reaching customers who prefer to buy artwork for a lower price or in a different format.
3. **Maximizing Profit**

- Diversifying your income can boost overall profits because you're making money from different channels. Some streams may have lower costs or higher profit margins than others, which adds to your bottom line.
- **Example**: A yoga instructor might offer in-person classes but could also create an online course. The course can be sold repeatedly without the need for additional work after it's created, generating passive income.

How to Create Multiple Revenue Streams

1. **Develop New Products or Services**
    - A simple way to add new revenue streams is by expanding your product or service offerings. If your business is known for one thing, think about related products or services you can introduce that customers would find useful.
    - **Example**: A bakery that sells cakes could start offering catering services for parties or weddings. This adds a new stream of income by serving customers with large events rather than just individual purchases.
2. **Create Digital Products**
    - One of the most effective ways to diversify your revenue is by creating digital products. Digital goods can be sold over and over again with minimal additional costs, making them a great way to generate passive income.
    - **Example**: A fitness coach might create downloadable workout plans or an e-book on healthy eating. Once created, these products can be sold online without the need for shipping or physical inventory.
3. **Subscription Services**
    - Offering subscription services can create a consistent, recurring revenue stream. Instead of customers making one-time purchases, they sign up for a regular service that provides ongoing value.
    - **Example**: A coffee company could start a monthly coffee subscription service, where customers receive new coffee beans delivered to their door each month.
4. **Affiliate Marketing**

- If your business has a large online following, you can leverage affiliate marketing by promoting other companies' products and earning a commission on each sale made through your referral.
- **Example**: A fashion blogger could partner with a clothing brand and earn a percentage of sales whenever their followers make a purchase using a special affiliate link.

5. **Offer Classes or Workshops**
    - If you have expertise in a certain field, offering classes or workshops is a great way to make additional income. Customers pay to learn something new, whether it's a skill or knowledge related to your business.
    - **Example**: A photographer could offer workshops on how to take better pictures, teaching photography techniques to both amateurs and aspiring professionals.

Key Considerations When Expanding Revenue Streams

1. **Focus on Your Strengths**
    - While it's tempting to explore many different revenue streams, it's important to stay focused on what you do best. Choose additional income sources that complement your business and align with your expertise.
    - **Example**: A clothing store might decide to start offering personal styling services since it fits well with their existing product line, rather than branching into unrelated industries like home goods.
2. **Keep an Eye on Costs**
    - Every new revenue stream requires some upfront investment, whether it's time, money, or resources. Make sure to calculate the costs involved and balance them against the potential profits. Start small, test your idea, and expand only when you're sure it will be profitable.
    - **Example**: A fitness trainer who wants to offer an online course should start with a few video lessons and gauge customer interest before investing in a full-blown course production.
3. **Test the Market**

- Before fully launching a new revenue stream, it's important to test the waters. See if there's interest in your new product or service before making a significant investment. This helps reduce risk and gives you time to refine your approach based on customer feedback.
- **Example**: A restaurant might try adding a few new dishes to its menu as a limited-time offer. If they're popular, they can be added permanently.

Expanding your business with multiple revenue streams not only helps you grow but also provides a safety net in case one part of your business faces challenges. By diversifying your income through new products, services, digital goods, and subscriptions, you can create a more stable and profitable business model. Just remember to start small, focus on what makes sense for your brand, and make sure to keep an eye on costs to ensure you're maximizing your profits in the long run.

Chapter 24: Strategic Partnerships for Revenue Growth

Building a business doesn't always have to be a solo journey. One powerful way to expand your reach and grow your revenue is by creating **strategic partnerships**. This means teaming up with other companies that share your goals or have similar customers to help each other grow.
In this chapter, we'll explore what strategic partnerships are, why they matter, and how to form effective collaborations to grow your business.

What are Strategic Partnerships?

A **strategic partnership** is when two or more businesses come together to work on a project or a long-term collaboration. These partnerships are designed to benefit everyone involved. The goal is often to combine strengths, reach new audiences, and create more value for customers.

- **Example**: Imagine a small coffee shop partnering with a local bakery. The coffee shop can sell baked goods from the bakery, while the bakery can offer coffee from the shop. Both businesses reach each other's customers and increase sales.

Why Strategic Partnerships Matter

1. **Expanded Reach**
    - When you team up with another business, you instantly gain access to their customer base. This is a great way to reach new audiences that might not have known about your brand before.
    - **Example**: A clothing brand might partner with a shoe company to create a special bundle or a joint promotion. This lets both companies introduce their products to new customers.
2. **Shared Resources**
    - By working with another business, you can share resources like marketing efforts, technology, or even space. This can save costs and help you grow more efficiently.
    - **Example**: A yoga studio and a fitness gym could share a marketing budget to promote a joint wellness event. This saves both businesses money and helps them reach fitness enthusiasts.

3. **Added Value for Customers**
    - Strategic partnerships often create new offerings that provide extra value for customers. When businesses combine their strengths, they can create unique experiences or products.
    - **Example**: A tech company might partner with a software company to offer a special bundle deal, giving customers access to both products for a lower price than if they bought them separately.

How to Find the Right Partner

Not every business is the right fit for a partnership. To create a successful collaboration, you need to find a company that complements your own. Here are some tips for finding the right partner:

1. **Look for Similar Values and Goals**
    - The best partnerships are built on shared values and goals. Look for businesses that align with your mission and target audience.
    - **Example**: If you run a sustainable clothing brand, you might want to partner with other eco-friendly companies that also care about the environment.
2. **Complementary Products or Services**
    - Your partner's offerings should complement your own without competing directly. This way, both businesses can benefit without stepping on each other's toes.
    - **Example**: A skincare brand might partner with a company that sells beauty tools. Both products work well together but aren't direct competitors.
3. **Customer Overlap**
    - Make sure there's a natural overlap between your customer base and your potential partner's audience. This ensures that both businesses gain new customers from the partnership.
    - **Example**: A health food store could partner with a local gym to offer discounts to gym members. Both businesses cater to people interested in healthy living.

Creating a Successful Partnership

Once you've found the right partner, it's time to create a partnership that benefits both businesses. Here's how you can ensure a successful collaboration:

1. **Set Clear Goals**
    - Both partners need to have a clear understanding of what they hope to achieve. Are you looking to increase sales? Reach a new audience? Make sure both parties are on the same page from the start.
    - **Example**: A bookstore partnering with an author for a book launch might set a goal to sell a certain number of books during the event.
2. **Define Roles and Responsibilities**
    - Make sure everyone knows what they're responsible for. Who's in charge of marketing? Who's handling customer service? Clarifying these roles helps avoid confusion later on.
    - **Example**: In a partnership between a hotel and a tour company, the hotel might handle booking the rooms while the tour company manages the travel logistics.
3. **Communicate Regularly**
    - Good communication is key to any successful partnership. Schedule regular check-ins to discuss how things are going, any challenges that arise, and ways to improve the collaboration.
    - **Example**: A food delivery service and a local restaurant might meet weekly to discuss feedback from customers and adjust their offerings if needed.
4. **Measure Success**
    - To know if the partnership is working, you need to measure the results. Set up ways to track success, such as sales numbers, customer feedback, or website traffic.
    - **Example**: A fitness app and a wearable tech company could track how many users sign up for both the app and the product as a result of their joint promotion.

Examples of Strategic Partnerships

1. **Nike and Apple**
    - Nike and Apple formed a partnership to create the Nike+ product line, which includes fitness trackers that sync with Apple devices. This partnership combined Nike's fitness expertise with Apple's tech innovation, providing a product that helps users track their workouts and health data.
2. **Starbucks and Spotify**

- Starbucks and Spotify worked together to create a music-streaming service for Starbucks customers. Spotify users could listen to curated playlists while visiting Starbucks, and the partnership helped Spotify reach new users while enhancing the Starbucks experience.

Strategic partnerships are a powerful way to grow your business by expanding your audience, sharing resources, and creating more value for customers. By finding the right partner, setting clear goals, and maintaining good communication, businesses can collaborate in ways that benefit everyone involved. Whether you're a small business or a larger brand, partnerships can be a game-changing strategy for increasing revenue and achieving long-term success.

Chapter 25: Passive Income Strategies

Creating passive income streams is a smart way for businesses to generate revenue without constant active effort. Passive income means making money while doing minimal ongoing work after the initial setup. While it does take some effort up front to build these streams, they can continue to bring in revenue over time. Passive income can help stabilize a business's finances and increase profits in the long run.

In this chapter, we'll explore various ways you can create passive income for your business, including digital products, courses, and memberships.

What is Passive Income?

Passive income is money that you earn without actively working for it on a daily basis. Unlike active income, where you get paid for the hours you work or the tasks you complete, passive income keeps coming in even after the initial work is done.

- **Example**: A digital product, like an e-book, can be sold repeatedly once it's created, without needing to spend more time on it after the product is launched.

Benefits of Passive Income

1. **Financial Security**
    - Having passive income streams can provide a steady source of revenue, even when sales from your main business are down. This creates more financial stability and reduces the risk of depending on just one revenue stream.
2. **Scalability**
    - Passive income streams allow you to earn money from the same product or service without having to do more work. Unlike active income, where you trade time for money, passive income allows you to scale your business more easily.
3. **Flexibility**
    - With passive income, you gain the freedom to spend time on other parts of your business or personal life. Because you don't have to constantly work to earn passive income, it gives you more control over your schedule.

Types of Passive Income for Businesses

1. **Digital Products**
    - Digital products are one of the most popular ways to generate passive income. Once you create a digital product, such as an e-book, software, or downloadable guide, it can be sold an unlimited number of times with no extra work needed.
    - **Example**: A fitness trainer might create a series of workout plans that customers can download for a one-time fee. The trainer doesn't have to spend additional time on these plans after they're created, but they continue to bring in money.
2. **Online Courses**
    - Online courses are a great way to share your expertise and earn passive income. Many people are willing to pay for courses that help them learn new skills, and once you create the course, you can sell it over and over again.
    - **Example**: A graphic designer could create an online course that teaches beginners how to use design software. Once the course is recorded and uploaded, students can purchase it without the designer needing to teach the same material repeatedly.
3. **Membership Sites**
    - A membership site provides ongoing value to subscribers, such as exclusive content, tutorials, or access to a community. Customers pay a monthly or yearly fee, and you continue to earn money as long as they stay subscribed.
    - **Example**: A marketing expert could create a membership site where subscribers gain access to monthly webinars, tools, and resources for improving their marketing strategies.
4. **Affiliate Marketing**
    - Affiliate marketing involves promoting other companies' products or services in exchange for a commission on any sales made through your referral. If you have a blog, social media following, or email list, affiliate marketing can be an easy way to earn passive income by recommending products you believe in.
    - **Example**: A tech blogger might promote a popular software tool on their blog using an affiliate link. Every time a reader clicks the link and makes a purchase, the blogger earns a commission.
5. **Advertising Revenue**

- If your website or YouTube channel gets a lot of traffic, you can earn passive income through advertising. Platforms like Google AdSense allow you to display ads on your site or videos, and you get paid whenever someone views or clicks on an ad.
- **Example**: A travel vlogger could earn money by displaying ads on their YouTube channel. Each time someone watches one of their videos and interacts with the ads, the vlogger earns revenue.

Steps to Build Passive Income Streams

1. **Identify Your Niche**
   - Start by thinking about the skills, knowledge, or resources you already have. What can you create that will provide value to your audience? Focus on a niche where you have expertise and a loyal following.
   - **Example**: A business consultant might create a digital product like a "Small Business Success Checklist" to help entrepreneurs organize and grow their businesses.
2. **Create High-Quality Content**
   - The success of your passive income streams depends on the quality of your product. Make sure whatever you create is valuable, well-designed, and easy to use or understand.
   - **Example**: If you're creating an online course, include video lessons, downloadable worksheets, and other resources that enhance the learning experience.
3. **Set Up an Online Platform**
   - You'll need an online platform to sell your products or services. You can use platforms like Shopify for digital products, Teachable for online courses, or WordPress for membership sites. These platforms make it easy to manage sales and deliver content to customers.
   - **Example**: A writer could use Gumroad to sell e-books directly from their website, making it easy for customers to purchase and download the books in just a few clicks.
4. **Automate the Process**
   - Automating tasks like payments, product delivery, and customer support can save time and make the passive income process smoother. Many platforms offer built-in automation tools to handle these tasks for you.

- **Example**: If you sell a digital product, set up an automatic email that sends customers a download link as soon as they complete their purchase.

5. **Promote Your Passive Income Streams**
   - Even though these income streams are considered "passive," they won't earn money without promotion. Use social media, email marketing, and search engine optimization (SEO) to drive traffic to your products or services.
   - **Example**: A fitness coach might promote their digital workout plans on Instagram with before-and-after photos of clients who have successfully used the plans.

Challenges of Passive Income

1. **Initial Time and Effort**
   - Creating passive income streams can take time and effort upfront. You'll need to invest time in planning, creating content, and setting up your platform. However, once everything is in place, the work required will decrease.
2. **Consistency in Promotion**
   - Passive income streams still require some level of active promotion to keep generating sales. You'll need to stay consistent with your marketing efforts to keep traffic coming to your site or platform.

Passive income strategies are a powerful way to increase your business's revenue without constantly trading your time for money. By creating high-quality digital products, online courses, or membership sites, you can build a stream of income that keeps coming in with minimal ongoing effort. Though it takes some initial work to set up, passive income can lead to more financial freedom and stability for your business.

Part 7: Social Media Marketing for Revenue Growth

Chapter 26: Using Instagram for Business Growth

Instagram is one of the most popular social media platforms in the world. With over a billion users, it's a powerful tool for businesses looking to grow their revenue and build a loyal following. Instagram is all about visuals—photos and videos—that allow businesses to showcase their products or services in creative ways.

In this chapter, we'll explore how businesses can use Instagram to increase their revenue by reaching new audiences, engaging followers, and promoting products. Whether you're running a small local business or a larger company, Instagram can help you connect with your audience in meaningful ways.

Why Instagram Matters for Businesses

1. **Visual Content Drives Engagement**
    - Instagram is all about visuals. People love to see beautiful, inspiring, and relatable images and videos. For businesses, this is an opportunity to showcase products or services in a way that captures attention and encourages interaction.
    - **Example**: A clothing brand can post stylish photos of their latest collection to give customers ideas on how to wear the products.
2. **Direct Access to Your Audience**
    - Instagram allows businesses to engage with their followers directly through comments, likes, and messages. This creates a more personal connection, allowing brands to build relationships with their audience.
    - **Example**: A small bakery can respond to customers' comments on their cake photos, helping to foster loyalty and build a community around the brand.
3. **Instagram's Large User Base**

- With over 1 billion active users, Instagram offers businesses access to a massive audience. This means there's a good chance that your ideal customers are already using the platform.
- **Example**: A fitness coach can reach potential clients looking for workout tips or inspiration by sharing exercise videos and motivational content.

How to Use Instagram to Grow Your Business

1. **Create a Business Profile**
    - The first step to using Instagram for business is creating a **business profile**. This gives you access to tools like Instagram Insights (which provides data on how your posts are performing) and the ability to run ads.
    - **Business Profile Perks**:
        - Contact buttons (email, phone number) for easy customer access.
        - Insights on how your posts and stories perform, including engagement metrics.
        - The ability to create promotions and boost posts to reach more people.
2. **Share High-Quality Visuals**
    - Instagram is a visual platform, so it's important to share high-quality photos and videos that show your products or services in the best light. Make sure your images are bright, clear, and well-composed to attract attention.
    - **Example**: A café could post well-lit photos of their food and drinks, showcasing the presentation and atmosphere of the space to attract customers.
3. **Leverage Instagram Stories**
    - **Instagram Stories** are short posts (photos or videos) that disappear after 24 hours. Stories are a great way to share behind-the-scenes content, limited-time offers, or quick updates.
    - **Example**: A clothing store can use Instagram Stories to announce flash sales, giving followers a chance to grab a deal for a limited time.
4. **Use Instagram Shopping**

- With Instagram Shopping, businesses can tag products directly in their posts. This makes it easy for followers to view details and make a purchase without leaving the app.
- **Example**: A beauty brand could post a picture of a model using their makeup and tag the products in the photo, allowing users to click and buy directly from the app.

5. **Engage with Followers**
   - Engage with your followers by responding to comments, liking their posts, and even resharing user-generated content (UGC). This helps build a loyal community around your brand and keeps your audience engaged.
   - **Example**: A small plant shop could reshare photos from customers who've posted pictures of the plants they bought, thanking them for the purchase.
6. **Collaborate with Influencers**
   - Partnering with influencers is a popular way to reach new audiences on Instagram. Influencers can promote your products to their followers, helping you gain more exposure.
   - **Example**: A skincare company might collaborate with a beauty influencer to review their products in a post or Instagram Story, encouraging their followers to try the brand.

Best Practices for Instagram Success

1. **Post Consistently**
   - Consistency is key on Instagram. Try to post regularly so your audience knows when to expect new content. You can also use tools like scheduling apps to plan and organize your posts in advance.
2. **Use Hashtags Strategically**
   - Hashtags help your posts get discovered by people who are interested in what you offer. Use a mix of popular and niche hashtags that relate to your business.
   - **Example**: A travel company might use hashtags like #TravelTips and #AdventureAwaits to reach people looking for vacation ideas.
3. **Host Giveaways or Contests**
   - Giveaways are a fun way to engage your audience and attract new followers. Offer a prize in exchange for likes, follows, or tags, which helps spread the word about your business.

- **Example**: A jewelry store might run a contest where participants tag friends in the comments for a chance to win a necklace.

Measuring Success on Instagram

1. **Track Engagement**
    - Engagement metrics such as likes, comments, shares, and saves are great indicators of how well your content resonates with your audience. Pay attention to what types of posts get the most interaction.
2. **Monitor Follower Growth**
    - Keep track of how your follower count grows over time. If you're seeing steady growth, it's a sign that your content is reaching and resonating with more people.
3. **Use Instagram Insights**
    - Instagram Insights allows you to measure post performance, track engagement, and see which types of content are most effective. Use this data to adjust your strategy and improve your content.

Instagram is a powerful tool for businesses to grow their brand, engage with customers, and increase revenue. By sharing high-quality visuals, interacting with followers, and using Instagram's unique features like Stories and Shopping, businesses can build a strong online presence. Whether you're promoting a product, service, or building brand awareness, Instagram offers endless opportunities to connect with a global audience and grow your business.

Chapter 27: Engaging Audiences on Facebook and YouTube

Social media platforms like Facebook and YouTube are not just for social interaction—they are also powerful tools for businesses. By using these platforms effectively, businesses can reach a large audience, build strong relationships, and ultimately drive sales. In this chapter, we will discuss how to use Facebook and YouTube to engage audiences and grow your business.

Why Facebook and YouTube Matter for Businesses

- **Large User Base**
    - Facebook has over 2 billion active users, and YouTube has over 2.5 billion users worldwide. This provides businesses with the potential to reach a massive audience, regardless of the size of their business.
    - **Example**: A small clothing store can advertise its new collection to thousands of people in its local area by targeting specific demographics on Facebook.
- **High Engagement**
    - Both platforms encourage high engagement through comments, shares, likes, and subscriptions. This allows businesses to interact directly with their customers and foster a sense of community.
    - **Example**: A tech company can post a product demo video on YouTube and respond to user questions in the comments, building trust and rapport with potential buyers.

How to Use Facebook for Business Growth

- **Create a Business Page**
    - A Facebook business page serves as the online presence for your brand. Here, you can share updates, products, promotions, and engage with followers.
    - **Example**: A restaurant can use its Facebook page to post daily menus, special deals, and upcoming events, encouraging customers to visit.
- **Utilize Facebook Ads**

  - Facebook's ad platform allows businesses to target specific audiences based on demographics, interests, and behavior. By investing in ads, you can reach people who are likely to be interested in your products.
  - **Example:** A fitness trainer might target people who are interested in health and fitness within a 10-mile radius of their gym.
- **Run Contests and Giveaways**
  - Contests and giveaways are a fun way to engage your audience and encourage them to interact with your business page. This can help grow your follower base and create excitement around your brand.
  - **Example**: A skincare brand might run a contest where participants tag a friend in the comments for a chance to win a free skincare kit.
- **Engage with Your Audience**
  - Regularly responding to comments and messages helps create a strong connection with your followers. Engaging with your audience makes your business feel more approachable.
  - **Example**: A local coffee shop might respond to a customer who left a positive review, thanking them for their feedback and offering a discount on their next visit.

How to Use YouTube for Business Growth

1. **Create High-Quality Content**
   - YouTube is all about video content. Whether you're demonstrating products, providing tutorials, or sharing behind-the-scenes footage, your content should be high-quality and valuable to your audience.
   - **Example**: A makeup artist might post tutorials on how to use different beauty products, offering tips and tricks that viewers find helpful.

1. **Optimize Your Videos for Search**
   - YouTube is the second-largest search engine in the world. By using the right keywords in your video titles, descriptions, and tags, you can help your videos show up in search results and attract more viewers.

  - **Example**: A cooking channel might use keywords like "easy dinner recipes" or "healthy meal ideas" to attract people searching for cooking tutorials.
- **Encourage Subscriptions**
  - Encouraging viewers to subscribe to your channel ensures that they'll see your new content in their feed. This helps you maintain a regular audience who is engaged with your brand.
  - **Example**: A fitness coach might end each video by asking viewers to subscribe to their channel for more workout videos.
- **Collaborate with Influencers**
  - Working with YouTube influencers can help you reach a wider audience. Influencers already have established followers who trust their recommendations, making influencer collaborations a powerful marketing tool.
  - **Example**: A gaming company could partner with a popular YouTuber who reviews video games, allowing the influencer to showcase their latest release.

Best Practices for Facebook and YouTube Success

2. **Consistency is Key**
   - Post content consistently to keep your audience engaged. On Facebook, this could mean sharing updates, videos, or promotions a few times a week. On YouTube, aim to upload videos regularly so that your audience knows when to expect new content.
   - **Example**: A travel vlogger might post a new video every Friday, creating anticipation and encouraging viewers to return each week.
3. **Engage with Your Community**
   - Engagement is a two-way street. Respond to comments, ask questions, and create content that invites interaction. This builds a loyal community around your brand.
   - **Example**: A tech company could post a Facebook poll asking customers what features they would like to see in the next product release.
4. **Use Visuals and Video Creatively**

  - Both Facebook and YouTube are highly visual platforms. Use high-quality photos, videos, and graphics to capture attention. On YouTube, be sure to edit your videos to make them visually appealing and engaging from start to finish.
  - **Example**: A fashion brand might post a YouTube video showing how to style different outfits for various occasions using professional editing techniques to keep viewers engaged.

Measuring Success on Facebook and YouTube

5. **Track Engagement**
   - Track metrics like likes, shares, comments, and views to see how well your content is performing. The more engagement your posts or videos receive, the more likely they are to be seen by a wider audience.
   - **Example**: A pet store might track how many people share their Facebook post about a new product launch to measure interest.
6. **Monitor Follower Growth**
   - Follower count is a good indicator of how well your content is resonating with people. Pay attention to how your follower base grows over time on both platforms.
   - **Example**: A fitness influencer might monitor how many new subscribers they gain after posting a viral workout video on YouTube.
7. **Use Analytics Tools**
   - Both Facebook and YouTube provide analytics tools to help you track your performance. These tools show you which types of content perform best, which can help you refine your strategy.
   - **Example**: A clothing brand might use Facebook Insights to see that their posts featuring customer reviews get more engagement, leading them to share more of that content.

Facebook and YouTube are powerful platforms for engaging audiences and driving business growth. By creating high-quality content, interacting with followers, and using the tools and features available on each platform, businesses can build strong connections with their audience and increase their revenue. Whether you're running a small local business or a larger brand, mastering these platforms can open up new opportunities for success.

Chapter 28: Measuring Social Media Success

When you're using social media to grow your business, it's essential to know whether your efforts are working. Measuring success on social media involves tracking specific metrics and using tools to see how well your content is performing. This allows you to make informed decisions on what to post, when to post, and how to engage with your audience. In this chapter, we'll discuss the key metrics, tools, and strategies to effectively measure your social media success.

Why Measure Social Media Success?

Social media can be a significant investment of time and sometimes money. By measuring your success, you ensure that you're getting a good return on that investment (ROI). Without tracking the right metrics, it's impossible to know if your social media strategy is driving sales, building your audience, or increasing engagement.

Benefits of Measuring Success:

1. **Evaluate the Effectiveness of Your Strategy:** Knowing which posts perform well helps you optimize your content.
2. **Understand Audience Preferences:** By seeing what your audience engages with most, you can tailor future posts to their preferences.
3. **Maximize Your Marketing Budget:** For businesses running paid ads, measuring success helps determine whether you're spending wisely.

Key Metrics to Track

1. **Engagement Rate**
   - **Engagement** refers to how your audience interacts with your content, such as likes, comments, shares, and saves. A high engagement rate means your content resonates with your audience, prompting them to take action.
   - **How to Measure It:** Take the total number of engagements (likes, comments, shares, etc.) and divide it by the number of followers or impressions (how many people saw the post). Multiply by 100 to get the percentage.
2. **Follower Growth**

- Tracking your follower count over time helps you see how fast your audience is growing. A steady increase in followers means more people are interested in your brand.
- **How to Measure It:** Monitor how many new followers you gain each week or month. Also, consider the quality of these followers—are they engaging with your content or just following without interaction?

3. **Click-Through Rate (CTR)**
    - **CTR** measures how many people clicked on a link in your post, leading them to your website or product page. It's a crucial metric for understanding if your content is driving traffic to your business.
    - **How to Measure It:** Take the total number of clicks on your link and divide it by the number of people who saw the post. Multiply by 100 for the percentage.
4. **Conversion Rate**
    - **Conversion Rate** is one of the most important metrics because it shows how many of your social media followers take the next step and make a purchase, sign up for your newsletter, or complete another desired action.
    - **How to Measure It:** Divide the number of conversions (sales, sign-ups, etc.) by the total number of clicks on your post. Multiply by 100 to get the percentage.
5. **Impressions and Reach**
    - **Impressions** refer to how many times your post was shown, while **reach** is the number of unique users who saw your post. These metrics help you understand how far your content is spreading.
    - **How to Measure It:** Most social media platforms provide this data in their analytics tools, showing how many users were exposed to your content.

Tools for Measuring Social Media Success

1. **Facebook Insights**
    - Facebook provides detailed analytics through its **Facebook Insights** tool. Here, you can track everything from page views and post engagements to follower demographics.
    - **Use it to:** See which posts are performing best, understand your audience, and track ad performance.

2. **Instagram Insights**
   - Instagram offers its own version of analytics for business accounts. **Instagram Insights** shows data on post interactions, follower growth, and website clicks.
   - **Use it to:** Determine which types of posts (photos, videos, stories) are most engaging and whether your audience is interacting with your content.
3. **Google Analytics**
   - If you're sharing links to your website on social media, **Google Analytics** can help you track how much traffic is coming from each platform.
   - **Use it to:** Measure the success of your social media campaigns in driving traffic to your website and converting followers into customers.
4. **YouTube Analytics**
   - For businesses using YouTube, **YouTube Analytics** provides data on watch time, subscriber growth, and engagement with your videos.
   - **Use it to:** Monitor which videos keep viewers engaged and lead to more subscribers or sales.
5. **Third-Party Tools**
   - There are many third-party tools, like **Hootsuite**, **Buffer**, or **Sprout Social**, that help businesses manage and measure social media success across multiple platforms.
   - **Use them to:** Schedule posts, track performance, and get detailed reports on all your social media accounts in one place.

How to Improve Your Social Media Success

1. **Post Consistently**
   - Consistent posting keeps your brand visible. Use a content calendar to ensure you're regularly sharing valuable content without overwhelming your audience.
2. **Engage with Your Audience**
   - Respond to comments, answer questions, and interact with followers. Engaging with your audience builds a community around your brand and fosters loyalty.
3. **Test and Learn**

- Social media is always evolving. Experiment with different types of content—videos, polls, infographics—and monitor which ones perform best. Use the data you collect to continually improve your strategy.

4. **Run Targeted Ads**
    - Paid ads on platforms like Facebook and Instagram allow you to reach specific demographics. By targeting the right audience, you increase your chances of engagement and conversion.
5. **Collaborate with Influencers**
    - Partnering with influencers in your industry can boost your reach. Influencers already have a loyal following, and their endorsement can introduce your brand to new audiences.

Measuring social media success is essential for any business that wants to grow its audience and drive revenue. By tracking key metrics like engagement, follower growth, and conversion rates, and using tools like Facebook Insights and Google Analytics, you can refine your social media strategy to achieve better results. Remember, social media marketing is a continuous learning process, so always test, learn, and adapt to keep improving.

Part 8: Leveraging Freelance and Contract Workers

Chapter 29: The Pros and Cons of Hiring Contractors

In today's business world, companies often rely on freelancers and contract workers for specific tasks or projects. These workers are hired for a short-term basis, and they are not considered regular employees of the company. Instead of being on the payroll, contract workers are responsible for their own taxes and benefits. There are many reasons why businesses might choose to hire contractors, but there are also challenges that come with this decision.
In this chapter, we'll look at the advantages and disadvantages of hiring contract workers and help you understand if this is the right choice for your business.

What are Contract Workers?

Contract workers, sometimes called **freelancers** or **independent contractors**, are individuals hired to complete specific tasks or projects for a company. They differ from full-time employees because they don't receive benefits such as health insurance or paid time off. Instead, they are paid for the work they complete, often based on a contract with a set duration and price.

- **Example**: A graphic designer hired for a three-month project to redesign a company's website is a contract worker. They are only responsible for completing the specific project and are paid once it's done.

Pros of Hiring Contract Workers

1. **Cost Savings**
    - One of the main reasons businesses hire contractors is to save money. Even though contract workers are often paid more per hour than full-time employees, businesses save on the costs of benefits like health insurance, retirement plans, and paid leave.

- **Example**: A small startup might hire a freelance writer to create content for their blog. They pay for each article, without needing to provide the freelancer with benefits like health insurance or vacation time.

2. **Flexibility**
    - Hiring contract workers allows businesses to adjust their workforce according to the amount of work available. If your company has a big project that requires more hands, you can hire contract workers for the duration of that project, and when it's over, you don't have to continue paying them.
    - **Example**: A retail company might hire extra staff for the busy holiday season, then let them go once the rush is over.
3. **Specialized Expertise**
    - Contract workers are often hired for their specialized skills. They bring expertise that may not be available within the company, and they can get the job done quickly and efficiently.
    - **Example**: If a company needs a new logo, they might hire a freelance graphic designer who specializes in branding rather than using someone from their in-house team who might not have the same level of skill in design.
4. **No Long-Term Commitment**
    - With contract workers, there's no obligation to keep them around once their work is complete. This allows businesses to scale up or down based on their needs without the complications of long-term employment contracts.
    - **Example**: A software company might hire a developer to create a specific feature for an app, but once the feature is built, the contract ends.

Cons of Hiring Contract Workers

1. **Less Control Over Work**
    - Since contract workers are not employees, companies may have less control over how and when the work is done. Contractors usually work on their own schedules and may not follow the same processes as full-time employees.
    - **Example**: A freelance marketer might have their own approach to social media strategy, which may not always align with the company's preferred methods.
2. **Lack of Loyalty or Dedication**

- Contractors are typically focused on completing the work and moving on to their next project. This means they might not be as invested in the long-term success of your company as full-time employees.
- **Example**: A freelance web developer might do an excellent job building your website, but they may not be available for ongoing support or updates after the project is done.

3. **Inconsistent Availability**
   - Since freelancers and contract workers often work with multiple clients, they may not always be available when you need them. If a contractor is juggling several projects, they might prioritize other clients over your business.
   - **Example**: A freelance writer could take longer than expected to deliver an article because they're working on projects for other clients at the same time.
4. **No Employee Benefits**
   - While it's true that hiring contractors saves money on benefits, it also means you don't have the ability to offer those benefits as an incentive to attract top talent. Some highly skilled workers might prefer full-time employment with benefits like health insurance, job security, and paid time off.
   - **Example**: A talented software engineer might choose to work for a tech company that offers full-time benefits rather than freelancing for multiple clients with no long-term job security.

When to Hire Contract Workers

Contract workers are a great option when your business needs temporary help, specialized skills, or when you want to save on costs. They are perfect for projects with clear start and end dates, or for tasks that don't require full-time attention.

- **Example**: If your company is launching a new product and needs a promotional video, hiring a freelance videographer to create the video makes sense, as this is a one-time project.

Hiring contract workers can be a smart business move when you need flexibility, specialized skills, and cost savings. However, it's important to weigh the pros and cons, especially if you're concerned about losing control over the work or the potential lack of commitment from freelancers. By understanding the advantages and challenges of hiring contract workers, you can make the best choice for your business needs.

Chapter 30: Virtual Assistants for Business Efficiency

Running a business requires handling many tasks, from answering emails and scheduling appointments to managing customer service and processing invoices. For many small businesses, these tasks can take up a lot of time and energy. This is where virtual assistants (VAs) come in. Virtual assistants are remote workers who handle administrative and operational tasks, helping business owners free up their time to focus on growth and strategy.

In this chapter, we will explore how virtual assistants can improve business efficiency, the types of tasks they can handle, and how to find the right VA for your business.

What are Virtual Assistants?

A **virtual assistant** (VA) is a professional who works remotely to provide administrative, technical, or creative assistance to businesses or entrepreneurs. Unlike in-house staff, VAs are typically hired on a freelance or contract basis, meaning businesses only pay for the time and services they need.

- **Example**: A real estate agent might hire a virtual assistant to manage their emails, set up client meetings, and handle basic social media posting.

Benefits of Hiring a Virtual Assistant

1. **Cost-Effective**
    - Virtual assistants are a more affordable option than hiring full-time employees. Since they work remotely, businesses save on office space, equipment, and employee benefits like health insurance or paid time off.
    - **Example**: Instead of hiring a full-time administrative assistant, a small business might hire a VA for 10-20 hours a week to handle tasks like scheduling and responding to customer inquiries.
2. **Increased Productivity**
    - By delegating routine tasks to a VA, business owners can focus on higher-level responsibilities like strategy, marketing, or product development. This increases overall productivity and allows for more efficient use of time.

- **Example**: A business owner might delegate bookkeeping and invoice processing to a VA, freeing up time to focus on meeting new clients.

3. **Flexibility**
    - VAs offer flexibility because they can be hired on a part-time, full-time, or project-based basis. Businesses can scale up or down depending on their needs without the long-term commitment of a full-time employee.
    - **Example**: An e-commerce store could hire a VA only during the holiday season to handle the increased volume of customer service inquiries.
4. **Access to Specialized Skills**
    - Many virtual assistants offer specialized skills, such as social media management, graphic design, or SEO (Search Engine Optimization). This allows businesses to access expert help without the cost of hiring in-house specialists.
    - **Example**: A small business might hire a VA with experience in managing social media campaigns to help grow its online presence.

Tasks Virtual Assistants Can Handle

Virtual assistants can take on a wide variety of tasks, depending on their skill set and the needs of the business. Here are some of the common tasks VAs can help with:

1. **Administrative Tasks**
    - Email management, appointment scheduling, answering phone calls, and data entry are standard administrative tasks that virtual assistants often handle.
    - **Example**: A busy executive might hire a VA to screen emails, respond to non-urgent messages, and set up meetings with clients.
2. **Customer Service**
    - Virtual assistants can provide customer support by answering questions, resolving issues, and processing orders. This is particularly helpful for businesses with online stores.
    - **Example**: An online retailer might hire a VA to respond to customer inquiries about shipping, returns, or product details.
3. **Social Media Management**

- Many VAs specialize in social media management, creating and scheduling posts, responding to comments, and tracking engagement metrics.
- **Example**: A small clothing brand might hire a VA to manage their Instagram account, post new product photos, and engage with followers.

4. **Bookkeeping and Invoicing**
    - Virtual assistants can handle basic bookkeeping tasks such as managing invoices, tracking expenses, and preparing financial reports.
    - **Example**: A freelance graphic designer might hire a VA to send invoices and keep track of payments.
5. **Content Creation**
    - Some VAs offer content creation services, such as writing blog posts, creating newsletters, or designing promotional materials.
    - **Example**: A VA might help a travel blogger by writing blog posts about popular destinations and sourcing photos.

How to Find the Right Virtual Assistant

Finding the right VA for your business can take some time, but it's important to choose someone who fits your needs and work style. Here are some tips for finding the right virtual assistant:

1. **Clearly Define Your Needs**
    - Before you start looking for a VA, make a list of the tasks you need help with. This will help you narrow down your search and find someone with the right skills.
    - **Example**: If you need help with social media, look for a VA with experience in managing social media accounts and creating engaging content.
2. **Check for Relevant Experience**
    - When hiring a VA, look for someone with experience in your industry or with the specific tasks you need help with. Ask for examples of their previous work and check references if possible.
    - **Example**: If you run an e-commerce business, find a VA who has worked with other online stores and understands customer service and inventory management.
3. **Conduct a Trial Period**

- It's a good idea to start with a trial period to see how well the VA performs and how they fit into your business. This allows both parties to adjust and determine if the working relationship will be successful.
- **Example**: You might hire a VA for one month to handle customer service tasks and evaluate their performance before committing to a long-term contract.

4. **Use Freelance Platforms**
   - There are many platforms where businesses can find virtual assistants, such as Upwork, Fiverr, and Freelancer. These sites allow you to browse profiles, read reviews, and hire VAs for short-term or long-term projects.
   - **Example**: A startup might use Upwork to find a VA who specializes in managing email marketing campaigns.

Hiring a virtual assistant can be a game-changer for businesses looking to improve efficiency and productivity. By delegating time-consuming tasks to a skilled VA, business owners can focus on growing their company and achieving long-term success. Whether you need help with administrative work, customer service, or social media management, virtual assistants offer flexible and cost-effective solutions for businesses of all sizes.

Chapter 31: Freelance Platforms for Hiring Specialists

In today's business world, more companies are turning to freelance platforms to hire skilled workers for specific projects or short-term tasks. These platforms connect businesses with freelancers, allowing companies to find specialists quickly and efficiently. Whether you need a graphic designer, content writer, or web developer, freelance platforms like Upwork, Fiverr, and Freelancer make it easy to find the right talent for your business.

In this chapter, we will explore how to use freelance platforms, the advantages of hiring through these platforms, and tips on finding the best freelancers for your projects.

Why Use Freelance Platforms?

Freelance platforms are online marketplaces where businesses and individuals can hire freelancers for various tasks. These platforms provide a convenient way for companies to find specialized talent for short-term projects without the need to hire full-time employees. Here are some key reasons why businesses use freelance platforms:

1. **Access to Global Talent**
    - Freelance platforms give businesses access to skilled workers from all over the world. This means you're not limited to hiring locally and can find the best person for the job, regardless of location.
    - **Example**: A startup in the United States can hire a web developer from India or a graphic designer from Europe through a freelance platform.
2. **Cost-Effective**
    - Hiring freelancers can often be more cost-effective than employing full-time workers. Freelancers are usually paid per project or by the hour, and businesses don't have to cover benefits like health insurance or vacation pay.
    - **Example**: A small business might hire a freelancer to design a company logo for a one-time fee, rather than employing a full-time graphic designer.
3. **Flexible Work Arrangements**

  - Freelance platforms offer flexibility in terms of work hours and project duration. You can hire freelancers for just a few hours or for an ongoing project.
  - **Example**: A company might hire a social media manager for a few hours a week to manage their Instagram account.

4. **Ease of Use**
  - Freelance platforms are user-friendly and allow businesses to post jobs, review freelancer profiles, and hire quickly. These platforms also handle payments, making it easier for businesses to manage the hiring process.
  - **Example**: A company can post a job on Upwork, review applicants, and hire a qualified candidate in just a few days.

Popular Freelance Platforms

1. **Upwork**
  - **Upwork** is one of the largest freelance platforms in the world, offering a wide range of freelancers for tasks such as writing, web development, graphic design, and marketing. Businesses can post jobs and invite freelancers to apply, or they can browse profiles and reach out directly.
  - **Best for:** Larger, ongoing projects and businesses looking for highly skilled professionals.
2. **Fiverr**
  - **Fiverr** is a platform where freelancers offer specific services starting at $5. It's ideal for businesses looking for smaller, more affordable tasks. Freelancers on Fiverr offer "gigs," which are pre-defined services with clear prices.
  - **Best for:** Quick, budget-friendly tasks like logo design, social media posts, or basic video editing.
3. **Freelancer**
  - **Freelancer** offers a similar range of services to Upwork, but it also allows businesses to run contests where freelancers submit work, and the best entry wins the job. This can be useful for creative tasks like designing a new product label or website layout.
  - **Best for:** Creative projects where you want to see a variety of ideas before choosing a final design.

How to Hire Freelancers on These Platforms

1. **Post a Detailed Job Description**
    - The more detailed your job posting, the easier it will be to attract the right freelancer. Include information about the project, the skills required, and your expectations for deadlines and deliverables.
    - **Example**: When posting a job for a content writer, include the number of articles needed, the topics, word count requirements, and any style guidelines.
2. **Set a Budget**
    - Freelance platforms allow you to set your budget based on hourly rates or a fixed price for the project. Be clear about how much you're willing to spend so that freelancers with the right qualifications can apply.
    - **Example**: If you need a logo design, you might set a budget of $100-$300 depending on the complexity and the experience level of the designer.
3. **Review Freelancer Profiles and Feedback**
    - Most freelance platforms allow freelancers to showcase their work through portfolios and reviews from previous clients. Take the time to review these profiles to ensure you're hiring someone with the right skills and a positive track record.
    - **Example**: If you're hiring a web developer, check their portfolio for examples of websites they've built, and read client reviews to see if they delivered work on time.
4. **Communicate Clearly**
    - Once you've hired a freelancer, maintain clear communication to ensure they understand the project requirements. Use the platform's messaging tools to discuss deadlines, provide feedback, and ask for updates.
    - **Example**: If you hire a video editor, be specific about the style, tone, and length of the video you want, and provide examples if possible.

Challenges of Hiring Freelancers

1. **Inconsistent Quality**

- One of the biggest challenges of hiring freelancers is the possibility of inconsistent quality. While many freelancers are highly skilled, some may not meet your expectations. This is why it's important to review portfolios and feedback carefully before hiring.
- **Solution**: Start with a smaller project or a trial run to test a freelancer's skills before committing to a larger project.

2. **Time Zone Differences**
   - If you hire freelancers from other countries, time zone differences can make communication difficult, especially if you need quick responses or real-time collaboration.
   - **Solution**: Make sure to discuss availability upfront and agree on regular check-ins to ensure the project stays on track.
3. **Limited Control**
   - Freelancers work independently, which means you won't have as much control over their work schedule or methods as you would with in-house employees.
   - **Solution**: Set clear expectations and deadlines, and maintain regular communication to monitor progress.

Freelance platforms like Upwork, Fiverr, and Freelancer offer businesses a convenient and cost-effective way to hire specialists for various projects. By posting detailed job descriptions, setting clear budgets, and carefully reviewing freelancer profiles, you can find the right talent to meet your business needs. While there are challenges like inconsistent quality and time zone differences, clear communication and defined expectations can help you get the most out of your freelance hires. Whether you're a small business looking for a quick task or a larger company needing specialized expertise, freelance platforms are a valuable resource for today's fast-paced business environment.

Part 9: Using AI in Business Marketing

Chapter 32: AI-Powered Customer Personalization

In today's fast-paced world, businesses need to find new ways to stand out and connect with their customers. One powerful tool that is changing the marketing game is Artificial Intelligence (AI). AI helps businesses create personalized experiences for their customers by analyzing data and learning about their behaviors. This means businesses can deliver content, products, and services that are more relevant to each customer, making them feel special and valued. In this chapter, we'll explain how AI-powered customer personalization works, why it's important, and how businesses can use it to improve their marketing efforts.

What is AI-Powered Customer Personalization?

AI-powered customer personalization is the use of artificial intelligence to tailor products, services, and marketing messages to individual customers based on their behaviors, preferences, and past interactions. AI gathers data from a variety of sources, like online browsing history, social media activity, and previous purchases, to understand what each customer likes and what they're likely to want in the future.

- **Example**: Think about streaming services like Netflix. AI looks at what shows and movies you've watched before, then suggests content you might enjoy based on your preferences. Similarly, e-commerce sites like Amazon use AI to recommend products you might like based on your browsing and purchase history.

How AI Personalization Works

1. **Data Collection**

- The first step in AI-powered personalization is gathering data about customers. This can include information like what websites they visit, what products they look at, and what they buy. AI systems collect data from customer interactions, social media platforms, websites, and apps.
- **Example**: A clothing store's website might collect data on what items a customer clicks on, how much time they spend on different product pages, and whether they add items to their cart.

2. **Data Analysis**
   - Once the data is collected, AI analyzes it to find patterns and trends. It looks at factors like purchase history, browsing behavior, and customer feedback to predict what the customer might want next. This allows the business to deliver relevant suggestions or personalized marketing content.
   - **Example**: An AI system for a bookstore might notice that a customer frequently buys mystery novels, so it will recommend similar books or new releases in that genre.
3. **Customer Segmentation**
   - AI also helps businesses group customers into different segments based on their behaviors and preferences. These groups can receive targeted marketing campaigns, making the content more relevant to them.
   - **Example**: A sports brand might use AI to segment its customers into groups like "runners" and "weightlifters" based on their purchase history, then send personalized email offers based on their interests.
4. **Real-Time Personalization**
   - AI can deliver personalized experiences in real-time. This means that as soon as a customer visits a website or opens an app, the AI can instantly provide recommendations, special offers, or personalized content.
   - **Example**: When a customer visits an online electronics store, AI can immediately show them products related to their previous searches or purchases, such as accessories for a smartphone they recently bought.

Why AI-Powered Personalization is Important

1. **Improves Customer Experience**

- Customers appreciate when businesses understand their preferences and provide them with relevant options. AI-powered personalization makes customers feel valued, leading to higher satisfaction and a better overall experience.
- **Example**: A customer who frequently buys eco-friendly products might receive personalized suggestions for sustainable goods, making them feel understood and appreciated by the brand.

2. **Boosts Engagement**
    - Personalization increases customer engagement because people are more likely to interact with content that is relevant to them. This can lead to more clicks, more time spent on the website, and a greater chance of making a purchase.
    - **Example**: A travel website that uses AI to suggest destinations and travel packages based on a user's past trips will see more interaction with those personalized recommendations.
3. **Increases Sales and Conversions**
    - When customers receive personalized product recommendations, they are more likely to make a purchase. AI can recommend complementary products (like matching shoes for an outfit) or offer personalized discounts, which encourages customers to complete their purchases.
    - **Example**: An online grocery store might use AI to recommend recipes based on items in a customer's cart, increasing the chances they'll add more ingredients to complete the recipe.
4. **Builds Customer Loyalty**
    - Customers who feel that a brand understands them and caters to their needs are more likely to return and make repeat purchases. AI helps businesses build strong relationships with their customers by consistently delivering personalized and enjoyable experiences.
    - **Example**: A coffee shop app that remembers a customer's favorite drink and offers a discount on their next purchase is likely to keep that customer coming back.

How Businesses Can Implement AI Personalization

1. **Invest in AI Tools**

- To start using AI-powered personalization, businesses need to invest in AI tools and platforms that are designed for marketing. There are many AI-driven software options available that can help with customer data analysis, recommendation engines, and targeted marketing.
- **Example**: E-commerce companies can use platforms like Dynamic Yield or Adobe Target to deliver personalized product recommendations and offers.

2. **Collect and Protect Customer Data**
    - AI relies on customer data to work effectively. Businesses need to ensure they are collecting the right kind of data, such as purchase history and browsing behavior. However, it's also important to protect this data and make sure it is used responsibly to maintain customer trust.
    - **Example**: Retailers might collect data on how often a customer shops and what they buy, but they must also follow data protection laws like GDPR to ensure customer privacy.
3. **Create Personalized Marketing Campaigns**
    - Businesses can use AI to create personalized marketing campaigns across different channels, such as email, social media, and websites. Personalized emails can include product recommendations based on past purchases, while social media ads can target specific customer segments.
    - **Example**: A beauty brand might send personalized emails to customers with skincare product recommendations based on their previous purchases and skin type.
4. **Monitor and Adjust**
    - AI systems continuously learn from customer data, but businesses need to monitor the results and make adjustments as needed. This ensures that the personalization remains relevant and effective over time.
    - **Example**: If a company notices that certain personalized offers are not resulting in conversions, they can tweak the AI's algorithms or adjust the type of recommendations being made.

AI-powered customer personalization is transforming how businesses interact with their customers. By using AI to deliver relevant and personalized content, products, and services, businesses can improve customer satisfaction, increase engagement, and drive sales. For any company looking to stay competitive in today's digital world, AI-powered personalization is a must-have tool.

ChatGPT

Using ChatGPT, or an AI language model (LLM), can be a powerful tool to boost your business success in many ways.

1. Brainstorming Ideas

- ChatGPT is like having a creative partner available 24/7. You can use it to:
    - **Generate new product ideas**: If you're looking for something fresh to sell, ChatGPT can give you ideas based on trends or customer interests.
    - **Come up with catchy slogans or taglines**: You can describe your business, and the model can suggest different ways to brand it.
- **Example**: Let's say you want to start a clothing line that inspires confidence. You can ask ChatGPT for slogan ideas, and it might suggest: *"Wear Your Strength"* or *"Confidence in Every Stitch."*

2. Market Research

- ChatGPT can help you **research industry trends, competitors, and customer preferences** quickly.
    - It can summarize key industry trends, so you understand where the market is headed.
    - It can also help identify who your competitors are and what they're doing, which helps you stay one step ahead.
- **Example**: If you sell art online, you can ask, "What are the trends in digital art sales in 2024?" and get an overview to help you align your products with current demand.

3. Crafting Emails and Pitches

- You can use ChatGPT to draft **professional emails, pitches, or proposals**. This can help you:
    - **Reach out to potential partners or clients** more effectively.
    - **Respond to inquiries** with polished, thoughtful replies.
- **Example**: If you're trying to license your artwork, you can ask ChatGPT to help you write a compelling pitch to a company. The AI can help you focus on what makes your art unique and why it's a great fit for their brand.

4. Social Media and Marketing

- Social media is key to building a brand. ChatGPT can help you:
    - Write **captivating posts** for Instagram, Twitter, or Facebook.
    - Generate **content ideas** for blogs or videos.
- **Example**: Say you run an apparel line. ChatGPT can help create posts like: *"Check out our new fall collection – designed to make you feel*

unstoppable!" It can even suggest ideas for blog posts like, *"How to Style Our Collection for Any Occasion."*

5. **Customer Support**
   - ChatGPT can help create **scripts for customer service** or even assist with frequently asked questions (FAQs) on your website. It can offer:
     - Fast, automated responses to common customer queries.
   - **Example**: If people often ask about returns or shipping, ChatGPT can help you set up an automated FAQ system that answers questions like, *"What is your return policy?"*
6. **Learning New Skills**
   - Running a business requires learning a lot of new things. ChatGPT can:
     - **Explain complex topics in simple terms**, like how taxes work or how to set up an online store.
   - **Example**: If you're not sure how to use certain software, like Photoshop for designing, you can ask ChatGPT, "How can I learn the basics of Photoshop for designing t-shirts?" and it'll give you clear steps or resources.
7. **Content Creation**
   - If you need help with **writing product descriptions**, blogs, or even generating new artwork ideas, ChatGPT can speed up the process.
   - **Example**: Let's say you want to describe a new hoodie you're selling. You can input the details into ChatGPT, and it might help you write: *"Our latest hoodie blends comfort with style, perfect for any occasion. Available in three bold colors!"*
8. **Boosting Productivity**
   - Sometimes you just need help staying organized. ChatGPT can assist with:
     - **Time management** by offering tips to streamline your daily tasks.
     - **Creating to-do lists** or offering reminders on key projects.
   - **Example**: If you're juggling product designs, marketing, and customer service, you can ask ChatGPT, "How can I organize my daily schedule to manage all these tasks effectively?"
   - By using ChatGPT as a tool for creativity, efficiency, and strategy, you'll find yourself saving time, making better decisions, and growing your business faster. The key is to treat it as a support system that can guide you through complex tasks while freeing up your time for other important things.

Chapter 33: Automating Routine Marketing Tasks

In today's fast-moving digital world, businesses are looking for ways to improve efficiency and stay ahead of the competition. One key tool for achieving this is automation through Artificial Intelligence (AI). AI-powered automation allows businesses to handle repetitive marketing tasks quickly and accurately, saving time and resources. In this chapter, we'll explain how AI helps automate routine marketing tasks, why it's beneficial, and the types of tasks that can be automated to make marketing operations more effective.

What is Marketing Automation?

Marketing automation refers to using software and AI tools to perform marketing tasks without the need for constant human intervention. These tasks range from sending out emails and managing social media posts to segmenting audiences and analyzing data. By automating these repetitive tasks, businesses can focus on more strategic goals like improving customer experiences and crafting creative marketing campaigns.

- **Example**: Instead of manually sending emails to hundreds of subscribers, an AI-powered tool can automatically send personalized emails to customers based on their behavior (such as visiting a website or making a purchase).

Why Automate Marketing Tasks?

1. **Saves Time**
    - Automating routine marketing tasks saves valuable time for businesses. Rather than spending hours manually posting on social media or scheduling emails, AI tools can perform these tasks automatically, allowing marketers to focus on other important aspects of their work.
    - **Example**: A small business owner can set up an automated system to schedule social media posts for an entire month in one sitting, freeing up time for product development or customer service.
2. **Increases Efficiency**

- Automation ensures that tasks are done quickly and without error. This boosts the overall efficiency of marketing operations by minimizing mistakes and ensuring consistency in delivering marketing messages.
- **Example**: An AI-powered email marketing tool can segment customers based on their preferences and send targeted messages without the risk of human error, such as sending the wrong email to the wrong group.

3. **Improves Personalization**
    - AI allows businesses to personalize their marketing efforts at scale. By analyzing customer data, AI can tailor marketing messages to meet individual preferences and behaviors, making customers feel valued.
    - **Example**: A clothing retailer can use AI to recommend products to customers based on their browsing history, offering them a personalized shopping experience.
4. **Enhances Data Accuracy**
    - AI systems are excellent at collecting and analyzing large amounts of data. Automation ensures that this data is processed accurately and used to make informed marketing decisions.
    - **Example**: A company can use AI tools to analyze customer feedback and reviews, identifying patterns that help improve product development and customer service.

Types of Marketing Tasks that Can Be Automated

1. **Email Marketing**
    - AI can automate the entire email marketing process, from sending welcome emails to follow-ups after a purchase. Businesses can set up triggers based on customer actions, such as signing up for a newsletter or abandoning a shopping cart.
    - **Example**: When a customer abandons their shopping cart, an automated email can be sent offering a discount to encourage them to complete their purchase.
2. **Social Media Scheduling**

- Social media platforms are crucial for connecting with customers, but managing multiple platforms can be time-consuming. AI tools can schedule posts in advance, automatically posting content at optimal times for maximum engagement.
- **Example**: A restaurant can schedule weekly posts about their menu specials and promotions on Instagram and Facebook, ensuring consistent social media presence.

3. **Customer Segmentation**
   - AI can analyze customer behavior and segment them into groups based on their preferences, buying habits, and demographics. This allows businesses to send personalized messages and offers to each group, improving marketing effectiveness.
   - **Example**: An online bookstore can use AI to segment customers based on their reading preferences and send tailored recommendations for new books they might enjoy.
4. **Ad Campaign Management**
   - Managing online ad campaigns can be complex, but AI can automate the process of bidding for ads, optimizing budgets, and targeting the right audience. AI tools continuously learn and adjust to improve the performance of the ads.
   - **Example**: A fashion brand can use AI to automatically adjust their Google Ads bids to target the right customers during peak shopping hours, maximizing their return on investment (ROI).
5. **Content Creation and Curation**
   - While AI cannot replace human creativity, it can assist in generating content ideas, writing basic copy, and curating content from other sources. This can help businesses maintain a steady flow of relevant content without overwhelming their marketing team.
   - **Example**: An AI tool can help a travel company generate blog post ideas about popular destinations based on current travel trends and customer interests.

How to Get Started with Marketing Automation

1. **Identify Repetitive Tasks**

  - The first step to implementing marketing automation is to identify the repetitive tasks that take up most of your time. This could be anything from sending out weekly newsletters to updating social media profiles.
  - **Example**: A small business owner might notice that responding to the same customer inquiries repeatedly is time-consuming. They can use AI to set up automated responses for frequently asked questions.

2. **Choose the Right Automation Tools**
   - There are many AI-powered marketing automation tools available, each offering different features. Research the tools that best meet your business needs and integrate well with your current systems.
   - **Example**: A company focused on email marketing might choose a platform like Mailchimp, while a business that heavily relies on social media might opt for Hootsuite for social media management.
3. **Start Small and Scale**
   - It's best to start with a few key tasks and gradually automate more as you become familiar with the tools. This allows you to fine-tune the process and ensure everything runs smoothly before expanding.
   - **Example**: A retailer might start by automating their email campaigns, and once they see success, move on to automating their social media posting and ad campaigns.
4. **Monitor and Adjust**
   - Automation isn't a set-it-and-forget-it solution. Regularly monitor the performance of your automated tasks and make adjustments as necessary to optimize results.
   - **Example**: If an automated email campaign isn't leading to conversions, a business can tweak the content or change the timing to improve performance.

Automating routine marketing tasks using AI is a powerful way to improve efficiency, save time, and increase the effectiveness of your marketing efforts. By automating tasks like email marketing, social media management, and customer segmentation, businesses can focus on strategic growth while providing a personalized experience for their customers. As AI technology continues to evolve, more businesses will adopt automation to stay competitive in the fast-paced digital landscape.

Chapter 34: Predictive Analysis for Customer Behavior

Predictive analysis is one of the most powerful tools in modern business marketing. It uses data, algorithms, and artificial intelligence (AI) to predict what customers are likely to do in the future. This chapter will break down how businesses use predictive analysis to understand customer behavior, why it is important, and how it can improve marketing efforts.

What is Predictive Analysis?

Predictive analysis involves using AI and machine learning models to study past customer behavior and predict what they might do next. Businesses collect data from their customers, such as their browsing habits, purchase history, and preferences. Using this data, AI models make predictions about future customer actions, such as what products they are likely to buy, when they might make a purchase, or how they might respond to specific marketing campaigns.

For example, imagine you have a favorite online store. Every time you visit, the website suggests products that seem to match your interests. This isn't a coincidence—it's predictive analysis at work. The website tracks what you've bought before and uses that information to show you similar items.

- **Targeted Advertising**: Companies like Amazon or Netflix use predictive analysis to suggest products or shows based on what you've previously bought or watched. The AI system predicts what content might interest you next, increasing the chances you'll stay engaged.
    - **Example**: After watching several superhero movies, Netflix might recommend more action-packed superhero shows, predicting you'll be interested in similar genres.
- **Inventory Management**: Retailers use predictive analysis to manage stock levels by forecasting demand. By analyzing past sales and seasonal trends, businesses can predict how much of each product to order, avoiding overstocking or shortages.
    - **Example**: A fashion store analyzes past holiday sales and predicts that winter coats will be in high demand during November, so they stock more of them in advance.
- **Churn Prediction**: Businesses often want to know if a customer is about to stop using their services. Predictive analysis helps by analyzing factors

like declining engagement or customer complaints, signaling that a user may leave unless targeted retention efforts are made.
    - **Example**: A mobile app notices you've been using it less frequently and predicts that you might stop using it entirely. To prevent this, it sends you a discount or a special offer to keep you engaged.
- **Dynamic Pricing**: Airlines, ride-hailing apps, and hotels use predictive analysis to set prices based on demand. By analyzing customer behavior and external factors like time of day or season, companies can predict when to raise or lower prices.
    - **Example**: When you book a flight, the system predicts that demand will be high over the holidays, so ticket prices increase. Conversely, during off-peak times, it predicts fewer travelers and lowers prices to attract customers.
- **Fraud Detection**: Banks and financial institutions use predictive analysis to detect suspicious behavior. By studying patterns in spending or transactions, AI models can flag anomalies that may indicate fraud and take preventive measures.
    - **Example**: Your credit card company notices an unusual transaction, like a large purchase in a foreign country, and sends you an alert or blocks the transaction, predicting it might be fraudulent based on your typical spending behavior.

Predictive analysis helps businesses anticipate customer needs, improve operational efficiency, and boost overall satisfaction by making smarter, data-driven decisions.

Why is Predictive Analysis Important?

1. **Personalized Marketing**
    - Predictive analysis allows businesses to create personalized experiences for each customer. Instead of sending the same message to everyone, businesses can tailor their marketing to individual preferences. This means customers are more likely to engage with the content.
    - **Example**: If a customer often buys sportswear, predictive analysis might suggest new athletic shoes or workout gear in the next email they receive from the store.
2. **Better Decision Making**

- Businesses can make smarter decisions by predicting customer behavior. They can invest in the products that are likely to sell well and create campaigns that resonate with their target audience.
- **Example**: A clothing store might use predictive analysis to decide how many winter jackets to stock based on how well they sold the previous year.

3. **Improved Customer Retention**
    - Predictive analysis helps businesses keep their existing customers. By predicting when a customer might leave or stop buying, companies can send special offers or reminders to keep them engaged.
    - **Example**: A subscription service might predict that a customer is about to cancel their membership based on a lack of activity. To prevent this, they might offer the customer a discount or bonus content to re-engage them.
4. **Optimizing Marketing Campaigns**
    - By predicting how customers will respond to certain ads or offers, businesses can optimize their marketing strategies. This means spending less money on ineffective ads and focusing on what works best for their audience.
    - **Example**: A business might use predictive analysis to decide whether to run a social media ad campaign or send targeted emails, depending on which method has been more successful with their audience in the past.

How Predictive Analysis Works

1. **Data Collection**
    - The foundation of predictive analysis begins with collecting vast amounts of data. Businesses gather data from various channels, such as customer interactions on their website, engagement with email campaigns, social media activity, and purchase history. This information is essential for building a comprehensive view of customer behavior. The more diverse and extensive the data collected, the more accurate and insightful the predictions will be. Predictive analysis thrives on this abundance of data because it allows AI to find patterns and correlations that humans might overlook.

- **Example**: Take an online shopping site as an example. This e-commerce platform monitors every action a customer takes—what products they browse, add to their cart, and eventually purchase. This data is collected and stored, enabling the AI to analyze customer preferences, popular items, and shopping patterns. This information lays the groundwork for predicting future shopping behavior, such as what a customer might buy next or when they're likely to make another purchase.

2. **Data Processing**
   - After the data is gathered, the next phase is processing it. During this stage, AI systems analyze and sift through the raw data to find meaningful patterns and insights. This involves breaking down the data into specific segments and categories, such as how frequently customers buy certain products, the times of day or seasons they prefer to shop, and their response to promotions or discounts. The AI looks for relationships between these factors, identifying trends that can be used to inform future actions.
   - **Example**: The AI might uncover that customers who frequently purchase running shoes often return within 30 days to buy related products like workout gear or accessories. Recognizing this pattern allows the business to anticipate these future needs. For example, the company could send these customers promotional emails about sportswear, predicting that they are likely to respond favorably and make another purchase.
3. **Predictive Modeling**
   - Once patterns and trends are identified in the data, the AI proceeds to build predictive models using advanced machine learning algorithms. A predictive model is essentially a mathematical formula that estimates the likelihood of future outcomes based on the data it has processed. The model examines a wide range of variables, such as customer demographics, shopping habits, and previous responses to marketing campaigns. Over time, as the AI ingests more data and refines its understanding, these models become increasingly accurate and sophisticated in predicting customer behavior.
   - **Example**: Imagine a customer who regularly shops during big sales, such as Black Friday. Based on their purchase history and behavior, the AI's predictive model might calculate that this

customer is more likely to make a purchase when offered a significant discount or during a limited-time promotion. This insight enables businesses to create targeted offers specifically designed to appeal to this customer, increasing the chances of a sale.

4. **Applying Predictions**
   - The final step in predictive analysis is taking action based on the AI's predictions. Once businesses have these insights, they can make strategic decisions that improve marketing, inventory management, and customer service. These predictions allow businesses to be more proactive, rather than reactive, in their approach. For example, they might adjust their marketing efforts to focus on customers who are predicted to make a purchase soon or optimize their stock levels to prepare for anticipated demand.
   - **Example**: A retail store gearing up for the holiday season might use predictive analysis to determine which products are likely to be most popular based on previous years' data and current trends. If the AI predicts a spike in demand for a particular product category, such as winter coats or tech gadgets, the business can stock up on these items in advance to ensure they have enough inventory to meet customer demand. This not only helps avoid stock shortages but also enhances customer satisfaction by ensuring products are available when needed.

By following these steps—data collection, processing, predictive modeling, and applying predictions—businesses can make informed decisions that optimize their operations and marketing efforts. Predictive analysis allows companies to better understand their customers, anticipate their needs, and stay ahead of market trends, ultimately driving growth and improving customer engagement. Through the smart use of data, businesses can be more agile and competitive, enhancing their ability to deliver personalized experiences and improve overall performance.

Benefits of Predictive Analysis in Marketing

1. **Higher Conversion Rates**

   - Predictive analysis helps businesses understand which customers are most likely to make a purchase, allowing them to target these customers with specific marketing campaigns. This leads to higher conversion rates—more people taking the desired action, such as buying a product or signing up for a service.
   - **Example**: A business might send personalized email promotions to customers who are predicted to be close to making a purchase, resulting in more sales.
2. **Reduced Marketing Costs**
   - Since predictive analysis allows businesses to focus their efforts on the customers most likely to respond, they can save money by avoiding ineffective marketing strategies. This means businesses can get more out of their marketing budget.
   - **Example**: Instead of sending a blanket ad campaign to everyone, a company can target only those customers who are most likely to be interested, saving on ad costs.
3. **Increased Customer Satisfaction**
   - When businesses use predictive analysis, they can offer customers products and services that are more relevant to their needs and preferences. This leads to better customer satisfaction and loyalty.
   - **Example**: If a customer frequently buys electronics, a business might recommend the latest gadgets, keeping the customer engaged and happy with their shopping experience.

Challenges of Predictive Analysis

1. **Data Privacy Concerns**
   - While predictive analysis can be highly effective, collecting customer data raises privacy concerns. Businesses must be transparent about how they collect and use data and ensure they follow data protection laws.
   - **Example**: Companies need to be upfront with customers about how their data is used and provide options to opt out of data collection.
2. **Accuracy of Predictions**
   - Predictive models are not always perfect. There's always a chance that the predictions could be wrong, which could lead to missed opportunities or wasted resources.

- **Example**: A business might predict high demand for a product and stock up, only to find that customer interest wasn't as strong as expected.

Predictive analysis is a powerful tool for businesses to anticipate customer behavior and make smarter marketing decisions. By using AI to analyze customer data, businesses can create personalized marketing experiences, improve customer satisfaction, and increase sales. However, businesses must balance the benefits of predictive analysis with the responsibility to protect customer data and ensure that their predictions are accurate.

Part 10: Creating a Comprehensive Marketing Plan

Chapter 35: Researching Industry Best Practices

To build a successful marketing strategy, it's important to first understand what works in your industry. By researching the best practices, you can create an effective plan that meets your business needs and speaks directly to your customers. This chapter will explain how to research industry best practices and why it's important to align your marketing efforts with them.

Why Research Industry Best Practices?

1. **Stay Competitive**
    - Every industry has specific trends and methods that companies use to succeed. By understanding these practices, your business can stay competitive and up-to-date with the latest tools, technologies, and strategies.
    - **Example**: If you run an e-commerce business, knowing how other companies optimize their checkout process or use social media advertising will help you keep pace with or even outperform your competitors.
2. **Understand What Works**
    - Best practices are often based on tried-and-true methods that have worked for other businesses in your industry. By following these methods, you increase your chances of achieving similar success.
    - **Example**: If you own a local café, learning how other small cafés use Instagram to attract customers can give you new ideas for building an online presence.
3. **Avoid Mistakes**
    - Researching best practices also helps you avoid common pitfalls. You can learn from the mistakes and successes of others without needing to experiment from scratch.

- **Example**: If you're planning a marketing campaign, researching similar campaigns that have failed can save you time and resources by avoiding ineffective strategies.

How to Research Industry Best Practices

1. **Use Online Resources**
   - The internet is full of valuable resources that provide insight into the best practices of various industries. Websites, blogs, case studies, and white papers often share helpful information and examples of what has worked for other businesses.
   - **Example**: Use platforms like HubSpot, LinkedIn Learning, or industry-specific forums to read case studies on successful marketing campaigns.
2. **Analyze Competitors**
   - A great way to find industry best practices is by studying your competitors. Look at their marketing strategies, customer engagement techniques, and the types of products or services they promote. This will give you an idea of what works and what doesn't.
   - **Example**: If your competitor is running a successful email marketing campaign, consider signing up for their email list to study how they interact with their subscribers.
3. **Attend Industry Events**
   - Trade shows, conferences, and webinars are excellent opportunities to learn from experts and hear about the latest trends. Industry events often feature presentations from successful businesses and leaders who share their insights.
   - **Example**: If you're in the fashion industry, attending fashion expos or listening to online panels about digital marketing for retail can give you up-to-date strategies for reaching customers.
4. **Use AI and Analytics Tools**
   - Artificial intelligence (AI) tools and data analytics platforms can help you understand what strategies are working best in your field. These tools analyze data from websites, social media, and sales to identify the most effective marketing approaches.
   - **Example**: Platforms like Google Analytics or SEMrush can provide detailed data on website traffic, keywords, and customer behavior, helping you refine your marketing plan.

Best Practices to Consider

1. **Know Your Audience**
   - The most successful marketing plans start with a deep understanding of the target audience. Know their interests, needs, and pain points to create marketing messages that resonate with them.
   - **Example**: If your business sells eco-friendly products, focus on customers who care about sustainability. Highlight the environmental benefits of your products in your messaging.
2. **Leverage Social Media**
   - Social media is one of the most effective ways to reach your audience. Use platforms like Instagram, Facebook, or TikTok to connect with your customers and showcase your brand.
   - **Example**: A local bakery might use Instagram to post daily pictures of fresh pastries, special offers, or behind-the-scenes videos, creating a stronger connection with their followers.
3. **Create Valuable Content**
   - Content marketing is a key strategy for attracting customers. By creating valuable, relevant, and engaging content, such as blog posts, videos, or social media updates, businesses can drive traffic and build trust with their audience.
   - **Example**: If you run a fitness business, writing blog posts on workout tips or sharing video tutorials can help attract new customers interested in health and fitness.
4. **Optimize for SEO**
   - Search Engine Optimization (SEO) helps businesses rank higher in search engine results, making it easier for potential customers to find them. By using relevant keywords and optimizing website content, businesses can increase their online visibility.
   - **Example**: A company that sells handmade jewelry should use specific keywords like "unique handmade jewelry" or "custom gemstone necklaces" to ensure their products appear in search results.
5. **Use Email Marketing**
   - Email remains one of the most effective marketing channels for keeping in touch with customers. Build an email list, send regular newsletters, and offer promotions to encourage customer loyalty and engagement.

- **Example**: An online retailer might send monthly newsletters featuring exclusive discounts, new arrivals, and personalized product recommendations.

Putting It All Together

Once you've gathered information on best practices, it's time to apply them to your business. Start by:

1. **Identifying Your Goals**
    - What are you trying to achieve with your marketing efforts? Define clear objectives, such as increasing website traffic, boosting social media engagement, or driving sales.
2. **Testing Strategies**
    - Try out different approaches based on your research. Whether it's using a new social media strategy or improving your website's SEO, testing helps you figure out what works best for your business.
3. **Measuring Success**
    - Track your marketing efforts with data and analytics. If a strategy is working well, consider scaling it. If not, make adjustments to improve your results.
4. **Continuing to Learn**
    - Marketing trends and best practices are always evolving. Continue to research and stay updated on the latest industry trends to ensure your marketing plan remains effective.

Researching industry best practices is a crucial step in creating a successful marketing plan. By staying informed about what works, learning from competitors, and using the right tools, businesses can develop strategies that resonate with their customers and drive long-term success. Make sure to continuously analyze and refine your approach to keep up with changes in the market.

Chapter 36: Step-by-Step Marketing Program Creation

Creating a solid marketing program is essential for any business looking to attract and retain customers. This chapter will walk you through the step-by-step process of building an effective marketing strategy. By following these steps, businesses can create a marketing program that aligns with industry standards, meets customer needs, and drives growth.

Why a Marketing Program is Important

Before diving into the steps, it's important to understand why a marketing program is necessary. A well-structured marketing plan helps businesses:

1. **Identify Target Audiences**: Knowing who you're trying to reach helps you tailor your marketing messages to attract the right people.
2. **Set Clear Goals**: With a marketing plan, businesses can outline specific goals, such as increasing brand awareness or driving sales.
3. **Allocate Resources Effectively**: A plan helps businesses use their time, money, and effort wisely.
4. **Measure Success**: A clear plan includes metrics to track performance, so businesses can adjust strategies based on what works.

Step 1: Define Your Marketing Goals

The first step in creating a marketing program is to set clear, measurable goals. These goals should align with your overall business objectives.

- **Example**: If your business goal is to increase revenue by 20%, your marketing goal might be to increase customer leads by 30%.
- **Tip**: Make sure your goals follow the SMART criteria: Specific, Measurable, Achievable, Relevant, and Time-bound.

Step 2: Know Your Target Audience

Understanding your target audience is crucial for creating a marketing program that resonates. You need to know who your customers are, what they want, and how they behave. This involves researching demographics (like age, gender, location) and psychographics (like interests, values, and lifestyles).

- **Example**: If you run a bakery that specializes in vegan pastries, your target audience might be health-conscious individuals or people with dietary restrictions.
- **Tip**: Use surveys, social media insights, and industry reports to gather information about your target audience.

Step 3: Conduct Competitor Analysis

Before creating your marketing strategy, it's essential to know who your competitors are and what they are doing. Competitor analysis helps you identify industry trends, best practices, and potential gaps in the market.

- **Example**: If your competitors are heavily using social media but you aren't, this might be a sign to boost your own social media presence.
- **Tip**: Analyze your competitors' websites, social media profiles, and marketing campaigns to understand their strategies.

Step 4: Develop Your Unique Selling Proposition (USP)

Your Unique Selling Proposition (USP) is what sets you apart from the competition. It's the reason customers should choose your product or service over others. Your USP should highlight what makes your business special and why customers should care.

- **Example**: If you own a clothing brand that uses only sustainable materials, your USP could be "Eco-friendly fashion for the conscious shopper."
- **Tip**: Keep your USP simple, clear, and focused on customer benefits.

Step 5: Choose the Right Marketing Channels

Not all marketing channels will be effective for every business. It's important to choose the channels that will reach your target audience most effectively. Common marketing channels include:

1. **Social Media**: Platforms like Instagram, Facebook, and TikTok are great for businesses targeting younger audiences.
2. **Email Marketing**: Sending regular newsletters and offers is an effective way to keep customers engaged.

3. **Search Engine Optimization (SEO)**: Optimizing your website to rank higher in search engine results can attract more traffic.
4. **Content Marketing**: Writing blogs, creating videos, and offering valuable information can attract leads and establish your business as an authority in your industry.

- **Tip**: Use a mix of marketing channels to reach your audience in different ways.

Step 6: Create a Budget

Having a clear budget for your marketing efforts ensures you spend your money wisely. A marketing budget typically includes costs for advertising, content creation, and digital tools.

- **Example**: If you're using Facebook Ads to promote a new product, your budget should cover the cost of the ads, as well as any additional content creation.
- **Tip**: Track your spending closely and adjust your budget based on what works.

Step 7: Develop a Content Strategy

Content is at the heart of most marketing programs. Your content strategy should outline the type of content you will create, how often you will publish it, and on which platforms.

- **Example**: A beauty brand might decide to publish tutorials and product reviews on Instagram, with a goal of posting twice a week.
- **Tip**: Focus on creating content that provides value to your audience. Educational, entertaining, and inspiring content is more likely to engage customers.

Step 8: Execute and Track Your Strategy

Once your marketing program is in place, it's time to put it into action. However, executing the plan is only the first step. It's important to monitor the performance of your marketing efforts to ensure they are meeting your goals.

- **Example**: If your goal is to increase website traffic, use tools like Google Analytics to track visitor numbers and engagement.
- **Tip**: Regularly review your metrics and adjust your strategy based on what's working and what isn't.

Step 9: Adjust and Optimize

Marketing is not a one-time effort. You should continuously analyze your results and make adjustments as necessary. This ensures your marketing program stays relevant and effective over time.

- **Example**: If a certain type of social media post gets more engagement than others, you can focus more on that content type in the future.
- **Tip**: Stay up-to-date with industry trends and customer preferences, and be willing to pivot your strategy when needed.

By following these steps, businesses can create a well-rounded marketing program that aligns with their goals, reaches the right audience, and drives results. A step-by-step approach ensures that every part of the marketing strategy is carefully considered and executed, increasing the chances of success. Keep in mind that marketing is an ongoing process, and businesses should remain flexible and open to changes as new opportunities and challenges arise.

Chapter 37: Action Plan for Growing Market Share

Growing market share means capturing a larger percentage of your industry's customers compared to your competitors. This chapter will guide you through creating a practical action plan to expand your market presence, helping your business stand out and dominate in your field.

Why is Growing Market Share Important?

Market share growth is critical for several reasons:

1. **Increased Profits**: A larger market share often leads to higher sales and profitability. When you attract more customers, your revenue grows, which can further be reinvested in your business.
2. **Brand Recognition**: The more market share you have, the more customers recognize your brand, which leads to better brand loyalty.
3. **Stronger Competitive Position**: Gaining market share weakens your competitors, making it harder for them to capture new customers.

Step 1: Analyze Your Market

Before you can grow your market share, you need to understand your current position in the market and your competitors. Start by asking:

- **Who are your main competitors?**
- **What are their strengths and weaknesses?**
- **What is your current market share?**
- Gathering this information will help you identify opportunities to outperform your competitors.
- **Example**: If your competitor has weak customer service, you can focus on offering exceptional customer experiences to win over their dissatisfied customers.

Step 2: Improve Product or Service Quality

To attract more customers and grow your market share, your product or service needs to stand out. Think about ways to improve the value of what you offer.

1. **Listen to Customer Feedback**: Customers will often tell you what they want if you ask. Use surveys, reviews, and direct conversations to learn what improvements you can make.
2. **Innovate**: Offer new features, services, or products that your competitors don't. Innovation can attract new customers and keep your current customers loyal.
3. **Solve Customer Pain Points**: Focus on the problems your customers face and solve them better than your competitors.

- **Example**: If you own a local gym and many members complain about overcrowding, consider offering off-peak discounts to spread out gym usage or invest in expanding your space.

Step 3: Optimize Your Pricing Strategy

Pricing plays a huge role in market share. If your prices are too high, customers might switch to your competitors. If your prices are too low, you may not make enough profit. Here are a few pricing strategies to consider:

1. **Competitive Pricing**: Price your products or services in line with your competitors to make sure customers don't leave because of price.
2. **Value-Based Pricing**: Charge based on the value your product provides. If you offer better quality or exclusive features, customers may be willing to pay more.
3. **Discounts and Promotions**: Use strategic discounts to attract new customers, especially if they've been loyal to your competitors.

- **Example**: A restaurant might offer a "new customer" discount to encourage people who typically eat at a competitor's restaurant to give them a try.

Step 4: Strengthen Your Marketing Efforts

To grow your market share, you need to increase awareness of your brand and attract more customers through smart marketing strategies.

1. **Targeted Advertising**: Focus on the specific audience most likely to become loyal customers. Use social media platforms, Google Ads, and email marketing to target these individuals directly.
2. **Content Marketing**: Create valuable content, like blogs, videos, or tutorials, that provides helpful information to potential customers. This positions your business as an expert and keeps customers engaged.

3. **Social Proof**: Showcase testimonials, reviews, and case studies from happy customers. New customers are more likely to trust your brand if they see others having a good experience.

- **Example**: A local coffee shop could run targeted Facebook ads promoting customer reviews to nearby residents, convincing them to visit instead of going to a large chain café.

Step 5: Expand Your Sales Channels

To reach more customers, explore different ways of selling your products or services. This might involve expanding your online presence or working with new distributors.

1. **E-commerce**: If you only have a physical store, creating an online store can help you reach customers who prefer shopping online.
2. **Partnering with Retailers**: Collaborating with retailers or distributors allows you to reach customers you wouldn't normally have access to.
3. **New Markets**: Consider entering new geographic markets or selling to new customer segments.

- **Example**: If your business sells handmade jewelry, you could start offering your products on popular e-commerce platforms like Etsy to reach a wider audience.

Step 6: Build Customer Loyalty

Keeping your existing customers loyal is just as important as attracting new ones. Loyal customers are more likely to recommend your brand to others and make repeat purchases.

1. **Loyalty Programs**: Reward your customers for repeat purchases through discounts or exclusive offers.
2. **Excellent Customer Service**: Provide quick, helpful, and friendly service to ensure your customers stay happy.
3. **Personalized Offers**: Use customer data to send personalized offers that make customers feel valued.

- **Example**: A beauty brand could create a loyalty program where customers earn points for every purchase, which they can later redeem for free products.

Step 7: Monitor and Adjust

Growing your market share is an ongoing process. It's important to track your progress and adjust your strategies as needed.

1. **Measure Success**: Track key metrics like sales growth, customer acquisition rates, and customer satisfaction to see if your efforts are working.
2. **Adapt Quickly**: If something isn't working, don't be afraid to change your strategy. This flexibility can help you stay ahead of your competitors.

Growing your market share involves a combination of understanding your market, improving your offerings, adjusting your pricing, enhancing your marketing, and expanding your sales channels. By following these steps and continuously measuring your progress, your business can become a leader in your industry and attract more loyal customers.

Part 11: Website Optimization for Marketing Success

Chapter 38: Crafting a Compelling Home Page

Your website's home page is often the first impression potential customers get about your business. It's critical to create a compelling and engaging home page that captures the attention of visitors and motivates them to explore further. In this chapter, we will explain how to craft a home page that draws in visitors, clearly communicates your business's value, and encourages people to take action.

The Importance of a Home Page

Your home page is like the front door of your business online. When someone lands on it, they need to know immediately that they are in the right place. If your home page is confusing or hard to navigate, people may leave quickly, which can hurt your business. A good home page should:

- Confirm to users that they've arrived at the right website.
- Create a strong first impression.
- Encourage visitors to explore other parts of your website.
- Guide users to take specific actions, such as signing up for a newsletter or making a purchase.

Step 1: Make a Strong First Impression

Visitors will form an opinion about your business in just a few seconds, so your home page must make a strong impression. Here are some key tips:

1. **Clear Message**: Communicate what your business does right away. In one sentence, explain how your product or service helps solve a problem or meets a need.
   - **Example**: A fitness center's headline could be, "Get Fit and Stay Healthy with Our Customized Workout Plans."

2. **Visual Appeal**: Use high-quality images or videos that represent your brand. These visuals should be clean, professional, and relevant to what you offer.
    - **Example**: A bakery might use mouth-watering photos of their best-selling cakes and pastries to make a connection with visitors.
3. **Easy Navigation**: Ensure your menu and navigation tools are clear and simple to use. Visitors should be able to quickly find the information they need.
    - **Tip**: Place key links, such as "Shop Now" or "Contact Us," in easily visible areas like the top of the page.

Step 2: Craft a Clear and Engaging Headline

The headline is one of the first things a visitor sees, so it needs to capture attention quickly. A great headline should:

- Be short and to the point.
- Communicate the unique value of your business.
- Encourage visitors to keep reading or take action.
- **Example**: If you run a subscription box service for pets, your headline might be, "Treat Your Pet to a Monthly Box of Surprises, Delivered Right to Your Door."

Step 3: Showcase Social Proof

Social proof, such as testimonials, reviews, or client logos, helps build trust with your visitors. When people see that others have had positive experiences with your business, they're more likely to trust your brand.

1. **Include Testimonials**: Share customer stories or quotes that highlight positive experiences.
    - **Example**: "I've never been happier with a gym membership—this place has it all! Highly recommend." — Alex, satisfied customer.
2. **Display Client Logos**: If you've worked with reputable clients, show their logos to demonstrate your credibility.
    - **Example**: If you provide B2B services, logos of your top clients can be added to your home page.

Step 4: Use Strong Call-to-Actions (CTAs)

A call-to-action (CTA) tells visitors what to do next. Whether it's signing up for a newsletter or purchasing a product, your CTA should be clear, specific, and compelling.

- **Examples of effective CTAs**:
    - "Start Your Free Trial"
    - "Shop Our New Collection"
    - "Sign Up for Weekly Tips"
- **Avoid vague CTAs**: Instead of saying "Learn More," try "Discover Our Services" or "Get a Free Quote."

Step 5: Optimize for Mobile Users

With more people browsing the web on mobile devices, it's essential that your home page is mobile-friendly. A poorly designed mobile site can lead to a high bounce rate, meaning visitors leave quickly.

1. **Responsive Design**: Your website should look and work great on both desktops and smartphones.
2. **Fast Load Times**: Ensure that your site loads quickly on mobile devices, as slow websites drive visitors away.

Step 6: Keep the Design Simple and Consistent

Simplicity in design helps users navigate your site easily. A cluttered page can overwhelm visitors and make them leave.

1. **Whitespace**: Don't be afraid to leave some areas blank. Whitespace helps highlight important content and makes your home page more readable.
2. **Consistent Colors and Fonts**: Stick to a consistent color palette and typography. This makes your site look professional and well-organized.
    - **Example**: A beauty brand might use soft pastel colors and elegant fonts to reflect its luxurious products.

Step 7: Provide an Informative and Engaging Portfolio or Product Gallery

Showcasing your work or products is key to convincing visitors that your business offers what they need. Display your best examples in an easy-to-navigate gallery.

- **Example**: If you're a photographer, your home page might include a portfolio with different categories, such as weddings, portraits, or commercial shoots.

Step 8: Offer Value with a Lead Magnet

A lead magnet is something valuable that you give visitors in exchange for their contact information. It could be a free eBook, a consultation, or a discount code. Lead magnets help you build your email list and stay in touch with potential customers.

- **Example**: A fitness trainer could offer a free "7-Day Workout Plan" in exchange for an email sign-up.

Step 9: Use Video or Multimedia to Boost Engagement

Video content can help explain your product or service in a more engaging way. It's a great way to showcase your brand's personality and connect with your audience.

- **Example**: A software company might use a video to demonstrate how their app works and the benefits it provides to customers.

A well-crafted home page is a powerful tool for attracting and engaging visitors. By using clear messaging, high-quality visuals, strong CTAs, and mobile optimization, you can create a home page that not only captures attention but also drives conversions. Remember, your home page is just the beginning of your visitors' journey—make it inviting, informative, and easy to navigate, and you'll see more users staying longer and becoming loyal customers.

Chapter 39: Enhancing User Experience Through SEO

Search Engine Optimization (SEO) is crucial for improving the visibility of your website and ensuring a positive user experience. In this chapter, we will explore how businesses can use SEO to make their websites more appealing to both search engines and users. By focusing on user experience and SEO together, businesses can drive more traffic, increase engagement, and convert visitors into customers.

What is SEO and Why Does it Matter?

SEO, or Search Engine Optimization, is the process of making your website more attractive to search engines like Google. When your website is optimized, it appears higher in search results, making it easier for potential customers to find you. But SEO isn't just about search engines; it's also about creating a great experience for the people who visit your site.

- **Example**: Imagine you search for "best pizza near me" on Google. The pizza places that show up first are likely those that have done the best job optimizing their websites. They have made sure Google knows their site is reliable and relevant to your search.

How User Experience (UX) Affects SEO

User experience (UX) and SEO go hand in hand. If your website is hard to navigate, takes too long to load, or isn't mobile-friendly, visitors will leave quickly, which hurts your SEO ranking. Google tracks how long people stay on your website, how many pages they visit, and whether they click on something or leave immediately (this is called the bounce rate).

1. **Website Speed**
    - A fast-loading website improves user experience and boosts SEO. People don't want to wait for slow websites to load. If it takes too long, they'll leave, and search engines will notice this.
    - **Tip**: Use tools like Google PageSpeed Insights to see how fast your website loads and get suggestions for improvement.
2. **Mobile Optimization**
    - More and more people are using their phones to browse the web. If your site doesn't work well on mobile devices, you're

missing out on a large audience. Google favors mobile-friendly websites in its rankings.
   - **Tip**: Make sure your site is "responsive," meaning it adjusts to fit different screen sizes, whether it's being viewed on a desktop, tablet, or phone.
3. **Easy Navigation**
   - Visitors should be able to easily find what they're looking for on your site. If it's too difficult to navigate, they'll leave, which can negatively impact your SEO. A clear, well-organized menu helps both visitors and search engines understand your site.
   - **Tip**: Group similar pages together and make sure every page on your site is no more than three clicks away from the homepage.

On-Page SEO Techniques to Enhance User Experience

On-page SEO refers to the steps you can take directly on your website to improve its ranking and user experience.

1. **Keyword Optimization**
   - Keywords are the words or phrases that people type into search engines when looking for something. By including relevant keywords in your titles, headings, and content, search engines can better understand what your site is about.
   - **Example**: If you run a local bakery, use keywords like "fresh baked goods," "custom cakes," or "best bakery near me" throughout your website.
2. **Title Tags and Meta Descriptions**
   - Title tags are the clickable headlines that appear in search results. Meta descriptions are the brief summaries underneath them. Both should include relevant keywords and be written in a way that encourages people to click.
   - **Tip**: Keep your title tags under 60 characters and your meta descriptions under 160 characters to ensure they display correctly in search results.
3. **High-Quality Content**
   - Content is one of the most important aspects of SEO. Search engines want to provide users with the best information, so the more valuable and relevant your content is, the higher your site

will rank. This includes blog posts, articles, product descriptions, and more.
   - **Tip**: Focus on writing content that answers common questions your audience might have. Keep your information up-to-date and use images, videos, and infographics to make it more engaging.
4. **Internal Links**
   - Linking to other pages on your website helps users find related content and keeps them on your site longer. It also helps search engines understand the structure of your site.
   - **Example**: If you're writing a blog post about wedding cakes, link to your product page where customers can order custom cakes.

Off-Page SEO Techniques to Improve User Experience

Off-page SEO refers to actions taken outside of your website that can improve its ranking, such as building backlinks and increasing social media engagement.

1. **Backlinks**
   - Backlinks are links from other websites to your own. The more high-quality, relevant websites that link to you, the more search engines will view your site as credible.
   - **Example**: If a popular food blog mentions your bakery and links to your website, this can boost your ranking and bring in new visitors.
2. **Social Media Engagement**
   - While social media itself doesn't directly impact your search rankings, having a strong social media presence can drive traffic to your website. This increased traffic can indirectly improve your SEO.
   - **Tip**: Share your blog posts, product launches, and special offers on social media platforms like Instagram, Facebook, and Twitter to drive more visitors to your site.

Monitoring and Improving SEO Performance

Improving your SEO is not a one-time task; it's an ongoing process. Regularly monitoring your website's performance will help you make necessary adjustments to keep it ranking high.

1. **Use SEO Tools**
    - Tools like Google Analytics and SEMrush provide insights into how your website is performing. They can show you which keywords are driving traffic, which pages are most popular, and where you can improve.
    - **Tip**: Set up regular reports to track your SEO progress and see how changes to your website affect your rankings.
2. **Adjust Based on Feedback**
    - Pay attention to user feedback and performance data. If visitors are leaving your site quickly or certain pages aren't ranking well, make adjustments to improve the experience and SEO.
    - **Example**: If a lot of people are leaving your site after visiting your homepage, consider revising the layout or content to make it more engaging.

Enhancing user experience through SEO is a win-win for both your business and your customers. By making your website easier to navigate, faster, and more relevant, you not only improve your search engine ranking but also keep visitors on your site longer. This leads to higher engagement, more conversions, and a better overall experience for your audience. Keep optimizing and improving, and over time, you'll see the results in both search engine rankings and customer satisfaction.

Chapter 40: Building a Website that Converts

Building a website that converts visitors into customers is crucial for the success of any business. In this chapter, we will explore what makes a website effective at turning potential leads into paying customers. Whether you're a small business owner or just getting started in marketing, understanding how to structure your website for conversion is key.

What Does It Mean to Convert?

A website conversion happens when a visitor takes a desired action, such as:

1. **Making a Purchase**: Buying a product or service.
2. **Signing Up for a Newsletter**: Joining an email list.
3. **Filling Out a Contact Form**: Requesting more information.
4. **Downloading Content**: Accessing a free resource, like an e-book.

The main goal of optimizing your website is to encourage visitors to take one of these actions, turning them into leads or customers.

Key Elements for a High-Converting Website

1. **Clear Call-to-Actions (CTAs)**
   - A Call-to-Action (CTA) is a button or link that prompts visitors to take a specific action. To make your website convert, you need clear and compelling CTAs on every important page.
   - **Example**: Instead of a vague "Click Here," use "Get Your Free Trial Now" or "Shop the Collection."
   - **Tip**: Place CTAs in visible spots, such as at the top of a page, at the end of articles, or next to product descriptions.
2. **Social Proof**
   - Social proof helps build trust. It includes things like testimonials, reviews, and case studies that show visitors that others have had a good experience with your business.
   - **Example**: Display customer reviews next to your product listings or a testimonial slider on your homepage. You can also showcase logos of companies that use your service.
   - **Tip**: Make sure your social proof is authentic and up-to-date.
3. **Strong and Clear Messaging**

- The messaging on your website should clearly explain what your business does and why it's beneficial to your target audience. Visitors should know within seconds what you offer and why they should care.
- **Example**: If you run an online tutoring service, your headline could be "Expert Tutors, Anytime You Need Them" with a subheading like "Personalized learning for every student."
- **Tip**: Use simple language and focus on the benefits your product or service offers to customers.

4. **Visual Hierarchy and Design**
   - A well-designed website uses visual hierarchy to guide visitors to the most important information first. This means structuring your pages so that key content, such as CTAs or product features, stands out.
   - **Example**: Use larger fonts for headlines and make sure your CTAs are in bold, contrasting colors.
   - **Tip**: Keep your design clean and avoid clutter. Use whitespace effectively to make your content easy to read.
5. **Mobile Optimization**
   - Many people access websites from their smartphones, so it's essential that your site works well on mobile devices. A mobile-optimized website adjusts to smaller screens and remains easy to navigate.
   - **Example**: Ensure that buttons are large enough to be tapped easily on a phone screen and that text is readable without zooming.
   - **Tip**: Use responsive design tools to automatically adjust the layout of your website based on the device being used.

Boosting Conversions with Persuasive Techniques

1. **Urgency and Scarcity**
   - Creating a sense of urgency can motivate visitors to act quickly. Limited-time offers or showing the number of products left in stock can push customers to make a decision.
   - **Example**: Display a message like "Only 3 items left in stock—Order Now!" or use countdown timers for sales events.
   - **Tip**: Be genuine when using scarcity tactics. If something is always on sale or running out, it will lose its impact over time.
2. **Easy Navigation**

- Visitors are more likely to convert when they can easily find what they're looking for. Organize your website so that important pages (like product categories or the shopping cart) are easily accessible.
- **Example**: Use a simple navigation bar at the top of your page that includes links to key sections like "Products," "About Us," and "Contact."
- **Tip**: Avoid using too many dropdown menus or hiding important links, as this can frustrate users.

3. **Consistent Branding**
    - Make sure your website's branding (colors, fonts, and logo) is consistent across all pages. Consistent branding creates a professional look and helps build trust with visitors.
    - **Example**: If your brand uses a blue color scheme and modern fonts, carry that style throughout every page to create a seamless experience.
    - **Tip**: Stick to a few key colors and fonts to avoid overwhelming your visitors with too many design elements.

Measuring Success and Improving Conversions

Once your website is live, it's important to track its performance. Here's how to measure and improve your conversion rates:

1. **Use Analytics Tools**
    - Platforms like Google Analytics allow you to track how many visitors are coming to your site and what actions they are taking. Use this data to understand which pages are converting well and which need improvement.
    - **Example**: You can see how many people clicked on your "Sign Up Now" button or abandoned the checkout process.
    - **Tip**: Set up conversion goals in Google Analytics to track specific actions, such as purchases or form submissions.
2. **A/B Testing**
    - A/B testing involves creating two versions of a webpage with one key difference, like a different headline or CTA. You can then see which version performs better and make adjustments accordingly.
    - **Example**: Test two different headlines on your homepage and see which one leads to more sign-ups.

- **Tip**: Test one change at a time to clearly see what is affecting your conversions.

Building a website that converts visitors into customers is all about clear messaging, strong CTAs, good design, and creating a positive user experience. By focusing on these elements and continuously testing and optimizing, you can create a website that not only attracts visitors but turns them into loyal customers.

Part 12: Paid Advertising Campaigns

Chapter 41: Targeting Facebook and Instagram Ads

In today's digital world, running paid ads on social media is one of the best ways to reach your audience. Facebook and Instagram are two of the most popular platforms for businesses to advertise because they offer a huge audience and powerful targeting tools. In this chapter, we'll walk through how to set up and optimize paid advertising campaigns on Facebook and Instagram.

Why Use Facebook and Instagram for Ads?

Both Facebook and Instagram have billions of active users, making them key platforms for businesses to find customers. What makes these platforms so useful is their advanced targeting options. You can choose exactly who sees your ads based on demographics like age, gender, location, interests, and even behaviors. This allows businesses to show their ads to people who are most likely to be interested in their products or services.

- **Example**: If you own a clothing store, you can target people aged 18-35 who are interested in fashion and live in your city. This makes sure your ad reaches the right audience, instead of wasting money on people who won't care about your business.

Step 1: Define Your Advertising Goals

Before you start creating ads, it's important to know what you want to achieve. Some common advertising goals include:

- **Increasing Website Traffic**: If your goal is to get more people to visit your website, you'll want to create an ad that encourages clicks.
- **Boosting Brand Awareness**: If your goal is to get more people to know about your business, you'll create an ad focused on spreading your message to as many people as possible.
- **Driving Sales**: If you want people to buy a product, your ad will need to highlight the benefits of your product and include a clear call to action (CTA), like "Shop Now."

- **Example**: A small café might want to run an ad that promotes a special weekend deal, encouraging people to stop by during the sale.

Step 2: Target the Right Audience

One of the biggest advantages of Facebook and Instagram ads is the ability to target a specific audience. You can use the following targeting options:

- **Demographics**: Target people based on their age, gender, education, job title, and more.
- **Interests**: You can show your ad to people who are interested in certain topics, such as fitness, beauty, or gaming.
- **Location**: You can focus your ad on people living in a specific city, region, or even within a certain radius of your store.
- **Behavior**: You can target people based on their online behaviors, like whether they've recently visited your website or purchased a similar product.
- **Example**: If you own a gym, you could target people who are interested in fitness and live within 10 miles of your location. This ensures that your ad is reaching people who are likely to sign up for membership.

Step 3: Create Engaging Ads

Once you know who you're targeting, the next step is to create an ad that grabs their attention. Facebook and Instagram are visual platforms, so your ads need to be eye-catching and engaging. Here are a few tips for creating great ads:

1. **Use High-Quality Images or Videos**: Ads with clear, bright images or engaging videos tend to perform better than those with text-heavy designs.
    - **Tip**: Show your product in action. If you're advertising a restaurant, show delicious food. If you're promoting a clothing brand, show people wearing the clothes.
2. **Write Clear and Simple Copy**: Keep your ad text short and to the point. Make sure people know what your business is offering and why they should care.
    - **Example**: "Get 20% off all online orders this weekend! Use code: SALE20."
3. **Include a Strong Call to Action (CTA)**: Your CTA tells people what you want them to do next. Common CTAs include "Shop Now," "Learn More," or "Sign Up."

Step 4: Set a Budget

Facebook and Instagram ads allow you to control how much you spend. You can set a daily budget (the amount you want to spend per day) or a lifetime budget (the total amount you want to spend over the life of the campaign).

- **Example**: If you only want to spend $10 per day, you can set that limit, and Facebook will make sure you don't go over that amount. This makes it easy for businesses of all sizes to advertise, no matter how much money they have to spend.

Step 5: Track and Optimize Your Ads

Once your ad is running, it's important to keep an eye on its performance. Facebook and Instagram offer detailed analytics that show you how your ad is doing. You can track things like:

- **Impressions**: How many people have seen your ad.
- **Clicks**: How many people clicked on your ad.
- **Conversions**: How many people completed a specific action, like making a purchase.
- If your ad isn't performing well, you can make adjustments. For example, you could try changing the image, adjusting the targeting, or increasing your budget to reach more people.
- **Tip**: Test different versions of your ad to see which one works best. This is called A/B testing, and it allows you to compare two ads and see which one performs better.

Running paid ads on Facebook and Instagram is a powerful way to grow your business. By targeting the right audience, creating engaging content, and tracking your results, you can increase your brand's visibility, attract new customers, and drive sales. Whether you're running a small local business or a large online store, Facebook and Instagram ads offer flexible options to meet your marketing goals.

Chapter 42: Google Ads for Business Growth

Google Ads is one of the most powerful tools available for businesses to grow online. This chapter will explain how Google Ads work, why they're effective, and how you can use them to drive business growth. By the end, you'll have a clear understanding of how to create effective Google Ad campaigns that target the right audience and increase your online visibility.

What Are Google Ads?

Google Ads is an online advertising platform developed by Google. It allows businesses to create ads that appear on Google search results pages and across the Google Display Network, which includes millions of websites. When someone searches for a keyword related to your business, your ad can appear at the top of the search results, helping attract potential customers.

- **Example**: If you own a bakery and a customer searches for "best bakery near me," your Google Ad could be one of the first things they see, directing them to your website or shop.

Why Use Google Ads?

1. **Reach the Right Audience**
    - Google Ads allows you to target people who are actively searching for products or services like yours. This makes it easier to connect with potential customers who are already interested in what you offer.
    - **Example**: A fitness center can target people searching for "gyms near me" or "personal training classes," ensuring their ads reach relevant customers.
2. **Cost-Effective**
    - One of the biggest benefits of Google Ads is that you only pay when someone clicks on your ad. This is known as pay-per-click (PPC) advertising. You can also set daily budgets, so you never spend more than you're comfortable with.

- **Example**: A small business with a limited budget can run Google Ads by setting a daily budget of $10. They only pay when someone clicks on the ad, making it a flexible option for businesses of all sizes.

3. **Measurable Results**
   - Google Ads provides detailed insights into how your ads are performing. You can track clicks, impressions (how many times your ad was seen), and conversions (how many people took action after seeing your ad). This data helps you fine-tune your ads for better results.
   - **Example**: If you notice that one of your ads is generating lots of clicks but no conversions, you can adjust the ad to make it more compelling.

How Google Ads Work

1. **Choosing Keywords**
   - Keywords are the words or phrases that trigger your ad to appear when someone types them into Google. It's essential to choose keywords that are relevant to your business and match what potential customers are searching for.
   - **Example**: If you own a pet grooming business, keywords like "dog grooming" or "cat grooming services" are ideal choices.
2. **Creating Ads**
   - Your ad is the first thing people will see when they search for your chosen keywords. It typically includes a headline, a brief description, and a link to your website. Your ad should be clear, engaging, and encourage people to click.
   - **Example**: A clothing store might create an ad with the headline "Summer Sale – 30% Off All Dresses" and a description that highlights the store's free shipping options.
3. **Bidding on Keywords**
   - Google Ads operates on a bidding system. You set a maximum amount you're willing to pay for each click on your ad. Google compares your bid to other advertisers, and the highest bidder usually gets the top spot in the search results.
   - **Example**: If you bid $1 per click and a competitor bids $0.75, your ad will appear higher in the search results than theirs.
4. **Targeting Your Audience**

- Google Ads allows you to target specific audiences based on factors like location, age, gender, and even the time of day. This ensures your ad reaches the right people.
- **Example**: A local restaurant might target customers within a 5-mile radius who are searching for "restaurants near me" during lunchtime hours.

Tips for Running Effective Google Ads

1. **Use Relevant Keywords**
    - Choose keywords that directly relate to your business. Think about what your potential customers are searching for and use those phrases in your ads.
    - **Tip**: Use keyword research tools like Google's Keyword Planner to find popular search terms related to your business.
2. **Write Compelling Ad Copy**
    - Your ad needs to stand out from the competition. Use action-oriented language that encourages people to click. Highlight any promotions, discounts, or special features that set your business apart.
    - **Tip**: Include a call to action (CTA) in your ad, such as "Shop Now," "Learn More," or "Sign Up Today."
3. **Set a Realistic Budget**
    - Start with a small budget and increase it as you see what works. Monitor your ads closely and adjust your budget based on their performance.
    - **Tip**: Set a daily budget to control your spending and ensure you don't go over your limit.
4. **Test Different Ads**
    - Don't rely on just one ad. Create multiple versions with different headlines and descriptions to see which one performs best. Google Ads allows you to run A/B tests to compare ad performance.
    - **Tip**: Try changing the headline or highlighting different benefits to see which version gets the most clicks.
5. **Monitor and Optimize**
    - Regularly check your ad performance and make adjustments as needed. If you notice certain keywords are costing too much without generating conversions, pause them or find alternatives.

- **Tip**: Use Google's automated bidding options to help optimize your ads for maximum performance.

Google Ads is a powerful tool for businesses of all sizes to attract more customers and grow their online presence. By using the right keywords, creating compelling ads, and targeting the right audience, you can drive more traffic to your website and increase your sales. Regularly monitor your campaigns and make adjustments to ensure your ads remain effective. With Google Ads, the possibilities for growing your business are endless!

Chapter 43: Crafting Effective Ad Copy and Design

When it comes to paid advertising, creating effective ad copy and design is key to grabbing attention and persuading people to take action. This chapter will walk you through the process of writing powerful ad copy and designing ads that convert leads into customers. We'll also discuss important elements like calls-to-action (CTAs), design principles, and ways to make your ads stand out from the competition.

What is Ad Copy?

Ad copy is the written part of your advertisement. It's the text that communicates your message and encourages your target audience to take action, such as clicking on an ad, buying a product, or signing up for a service.

- **Example**: If you see an ad that says, "Limited Time Offer! Buy 1 Get 1 Free—Shop Now!" the text you're reading is the ad copy.

Key Elements of Effective Ad Copy

1. **Attention-Grabbing Headline**
    - The first thing people see in an ad is the headline. A strong, attention-grabbing headline is critical to getting people to stop scrolling or looking elsewhere.
    - **Tip**: Keep it short and direct. Use phrases like "Limited Offer," "Exclusive Deal," or "50% Off" to draw people in.
2. **Clear and Concise Messaging**
    - Your ad copy should quickly explain what your product or service is and why people need it. Most people won't spend more than a few seconds reading, so make sure your message is clear and easy to understand.
    - **Example**: "Stay warm this winter with our premium wool coats. Free shipping on orders over $50."
3. **Benefits Over Features**
    - While it's important to mention what your product or service does, focusing on how it benefits your audience is even more effective. People want to know how your product will improve their lives.

- **Example**: Instead of saying, "Our shoes are made from durable materials," try "Our shoes are built to last, so you can enjoy comfort and style for years."

4. **Strong Call-to-Action (CTA)**
   - Every ad needs a clear CTA that tells people what you want them to do next. Whether it's "Buy Now," "Learn More," or "Sign Up Today," the CTA should be easy to spot and act on.
   - **Tip**: Create a sense of urgency with your CTA by using phrases like "Hurry! Offer Ends Soon" or "Only a Few Left in Stock."

Designing Eye-Catching Ads

The design of your ad is just as important as the words. The way your ad looks can impact whether or not people stop to read it. Let's go over the elements of an effective ad design.

1. **Visual Appeal**
   - People are naturally drawn to visuals, so using high-quality images or graphics is essential. Choose visuals that represent your product or service and align with your brand's message.
   - **Tip**: Avoid clutter. Keep your ad clean and focused on one main image or visual element.
2. **Use of Colors**
   - Colors can evoke emotions and influence how people perceive your brand. For example, red often creates a sense of urgency, while blue is associated with trust and calm.
   - **Tip**: Use contrasting colors for your CTA buttons to make them stand out from the rest of the design.
3. **Typography**
   - The fonts you choose can affect the readability of your ad. Make sure to use bold, easy-to-read fonts for headlines and important messages.
   - **Tip**: Limit your use of different fonts to avoid making the ad look chaotic. Stick to two or three complementary fonts.
4. **Consistency with Brand Identity**
   - Your ad design should align with your overall brand identity. This includes using your brand's colors, fonts, and logo in a consistent way across all ads.
   - **Example**: If your brand is known for luxury, your ad design should reflect that by using sleek, modern visuals and fonts.

Crafting Ads for Different Platforms

Each advertising platform, whether it's Facebook, Instagram, Google, or YouTube, has its own format and audience. It's important to tailor your ad copy and design to match the platform you're using.

1. **Facebook and Instagram Ads**
    - These platforms are visually-driven, so images and videos are key. Make sure your ad looks great on mobile since many users will see it on their phones.
    - **Example**: Use Instagram Stories to show short, engaging video ads with swipe-up CTAs.
2. **Google Ads**
    - Google Ads are text-based, so your copy needs to be compelling and to the point. Focus on keywords and phrases that will get your ad noticed in search results.
    - **Tip**: Include your main keyword in the headline to improve visibility.
3. **YouTube Ads**
    - Video ads on YouTube should be short and impactful. You only have a few seconds to grab attention, so make sure your message comes across quickly.
    - **Tip**: Use subtitles to ensure your message is understood even if viewers have their sound off.

Testing and Optimizing Ads

It's important to test different versions of your ad to see what works best. This process is called A/B testing, where you create two or more versions of an ad with slight differences (such as different headlines or images) and see which one performs better.

1. **Track Metrics**
    - Keep an eye on important metrics like click-through rates (CTR), conversion rates, and return on investment (ROI). These will help you understand how well your ads are performing.
2. **Make Adjustments**
    - Based on your results, adjust your ad copy, design, or CTA to improve performance. For example, if an ad isn't getting many clicks, try changing the headline or testing a new image.

Crafting effective ad copy and design is about balancing creativity with clear communication. By focusing on a strong headline, clear messaging, visual appeal, and a compelling CTA, you can create ads that not only grab attention but also drive action. Always remember to test different versions and adjust your approach based on performance data to maximize the impact of your advertising campaigns.

Part 13: Customer Acquisition and Retention

Chapter 44: Attracting New Customers with Digital Marketing

Attracting new customers is a key goal for any business. In today's world, digital marketing offers a powerful way to reach potential customers, build brand awareness, and drive sales. In this chapter, we'll cover the essential techniques that businesses can use to attract new customers using digital marketing strategies.

Why Digital Marketing is Important for Customer Acquisition

Digital marketing allows businesses to reach a wide audience, often at a lower cost compared to traditional marketing methods. By leveraging online tools and platforms, businesses can create targeted campaigns that engage potential customers based on their interests, behaviors, and demographics.

1. **Cost-Effective**: Compared to traditional marketing like print or TV ads, digital marketing is more affordable and offers a higher return on investment (ROI).
2. **Wide Reach**: The internet connects businesses with millions of potential customers globally, making it easier to expand your customer base.
3. **Measurable Results**: Digital marketing tools provide real-time data, allowing businesses to track the effectiveness of their campaigns and make adjustments to improve performance.

Key Digital Marketing Strategies to Attract Customers

1. **Search Engine Optimization (SEO)**

- SEO is the practice of optimizing your website to rank higher in search engine results. When customers search for products or services related to your business, your goal is to appear at the top of the results.
- **Example**: A bakery can use SEO to rank higher when customers search for "best cakes near me" or "custom birthday cakes."

2. **Key Steps for SEO:**
    - Use relevant keywords in your website content, titles, and meta descriptions.
    - Optimize your website for mobile use and fast loading times.
    - Regularly create high-quality content, such as blog posts or tutorials, to engage visitors and improve your ranking.
3. **Social Media Marketing**
    - Social media platforms like Instagram, Facebook, and TikTok allow businesses to engage directly with potential customers. By creating engaging content, businesses can attract followers who may eventually become customers.
    - **Example**: A fitness brand could use Instagram to post workout tips, user testimonials, and special promotions to attract health-conscious consumers.
4. **Key Tips for Social Media:**
    - Post consistently and engage with your audience by responding to comments and messages.
    - Use paid social media ads to target specific demographics, such as age, location, and interests.
    - Run contests or giveaways to encourage followers to share your content and attract more potential customers.
5. **Content Marketing**
    - Content marketing involves creating valuable, relevant content that helps your target audience solve problems or learn new things. By providing useful information, businesses can attract potential customers and build trust with them.
    - **Example**: A real estate company could create blog posts or videos about home-buying tips, which can attract people looking to buy a home.
6. **Content Marketing Tips:**
    - Create blog posts, videos, infographics, or eBooks that provide valuable information to your audience.
    - Share your content on social media and email newsletters to increase its reach.

- Focus on content that answers common questions or solves problems for your audience.

7. **Email Marketing**
   - Email marketing is a direct way to reach potential customers by sending them personalized messages, promotions, and updates. It's one of the most effective ways to nurture leads and encourage them to make a purchase.
   - **Example**: A clothing store could send out a weekly newsletter featuring new arrivals, special discounts, and styling tips to engage potential customers.
8. **Best Practices for Email Marketing:**
   - Build an email list by offering something valuable in return, like a free guide or discount.
   - Personalize your emails by addressing the recipient by name and sending offers based on their preferences or browsing history.
   - Use clear and compelling subject lines to increase open rates.
9. **Pay-Per-Click (PPC) Advertising**
   - PPC is a form of digital advertising where businesses pay for their ads to appear in search engine results or on websites. Every time someone clicks on your ad, you pay a fee.
   - **Example**: A travel agency could use Google Ads to appear at the top of search results when people look for "best vacation packages."
10. **How to Use PPC Effectively:**
    - Choose the right keywords to target. These should be relevant to your products or services.
    - Set a budget that aligns with your marketing goals and the potential value of each customer.
    - Continuously monitor and adjust your ad campaigns based on performance data to get the best results.

Tips for Maximizing Customer Acquisition

1. **Target the Right Audience**
   - It's important to focus your marketing efforts on the people most likely to become your customers. Use tools like Google Analytics and social media insights to understand your audience's behavior and tailor your marketing messages to meet their needs.

2. **Create a Compelling Offer**
    - Attracting new customers often requires offering something of value, whether it's a discount, free trial, or exclusive content. Make sure your offer is clear, attractive, and easy to redeem.
3. **Use Customer Testimonials and Reviews**
    - Social proof, such as testimonials and reviews, can help build trust with potential customers. Highlighting positive feedback from current customers can encourage others to try your products or services.
4. **Retarget Potential Customers**
    - Retargeting involves showing ads to people who have previously visited your website but didn't make a purchase. This can remind them of your products and encourage them to return to complete their purchase.

Attracting new customers with digital marketing requires a mix of strategies, from optimizing your website for search engines to creating engaging social media content. By using these tools effectively and targeting the right audience, businesses can grow their customer base and increase sales. The key is to experiment with different approaches, measure the results, and adjust your strategies to keep improving over time.

Chapter 45: Encouraging Repeat Business

To build a successful business, it's not enough to just acquire new customers. You also need to keep your existing customers coming back. This chapter focuses on strategies to encourage repeat business, helping businesses build long-term relationships with their customers.

Why Repeat Business is Important

1. **Lower Cost**: It's generally much cheaper to retain an existing customer than to attract a new one. Once you've already earned a customer's trust, they are more likely to continue purchasing from you without needing as much marketing or promotion.
2. **Increased Profits**: Returning customers tend to spend more on subsequent purchases. As they become more familiar with your brand, they may explore more products or services, increasing their overall lifetime value to your business.
3. **Word-of-Mouth Marketing**: Satisfied repeat customers are more likely to recommend your business to friends and family. This creates a cycle of referrals, leading to even more customers without additional marketing costs.

Strategies to Encourage Repeat Business

1. **Create a Loyalty Program**
    - A loyalty program rewards your customers for making repeat purchases, giving them incentives to come back to your business. Loyalty programs often work by offering points for every purchase, which can be redeemed for discounts or free products.
    - **Example**: A coffee shop might offer a punch card where customers get a free drink after purchasing ten drinks. This not only encourages customers to return but also gives them a goal to work toward.
2. **Tips for Building a Loyalty Program:**
    - Make it simple and easy for customers to understand and use.
    - Offer rewards that are relevant and valuable to your customers.
    - Use technology, such as apps, to track points and rewards efficiently.

3. **Personalized Offers**
    - Sending personalized offers based on a customer's previous purchases can make them feel valued and encourage them to return. Use customer data to send tailored promotions or discounts on products they've shown interest in before.
    - **Example**: An online clothing store could send an email to a customer who frequently buys athletic wear, offering a discount on new arrivals in their preferred category.
4. **Tips for Personalization:**
    - Collect data on customer preferences, such as their favorite products or shopping habits.
    - Use automated email systems to send personalized promotions based on customer behavior.
5. **Exceptional Customer Service**
    - Providing excellent customer service is one of the most effective ways to ensure customers come back. Respond to inquiries promptly, handle issues with care, and always aim to leave your customers feeling satisfied.
    - **Example**: If a customer has a problem with a product, offering a quick refund or exchange with a friendly approach can turn a negative experience into a positive one.
6. **Customer Service Best Practices:**
    - Train staff to handle complaints professionally and empathetically.
    - Ensure that your return policies are clear, fair, and easy to follow.
7. **Regular Communication**
    - Staying in touch with your customers through newsletters, social media, or personalized emails can keep your brand on their minds. Regular updates about new products, sales, or special events give customers a reason to come back.
    - **Example**: A cosmetics company could send out a monthly newsletter highlighting new makeup releases, skincare tips, and special promotions.
8. **How to Keep Customers Engaged:**
    - Use email marketing to share relevant content and updates.
    - Engage with customers on social media by responding to comments and messages.

- Keep your communication frequent but not overwhelming—aim for consistency rather than bombarding customers with too many emails.

The Role of Consistency in Repeat Business

Consistency in both product quality and customer experience plays a key role in encouraging repeat business. Customers need to know they can rely on you to provide the same high level of service and quality every time they shop.

1. **Consistent Product Quality**
   - Customers are more likely to return if they know they can expect the same high-quality products each time. Focus on maintaining quality across all aspects of your business, from the products themselves to the packaging and delivery.
2. **Consistent Customer Experience**
   - Whether a customer interacts with your business in person, over the phone, or online, they should always have a positive and consistent experience. Standardizing your processes ensures that no matter how customers interact with you, they receive the same excellent service.

Example: If you run a restaurant, the dining experience should be just as pleasant whether a customer comes in on a busy Friday night or a quiet Tuesday afternoon.

Measuring Success

Tracking the success of your efforts to encourage repeat business is essential. Use data analytics to monitor customer behavior and identify trends in repeat purchases.

1. **Key Metrics to Track:**
   - **Customer Retention Rate**: The percentage of customers who return to your business after their first purchase.
   - **Repeat Purchase Rate**: The percentage of customers who make more than one purchase over a set period.
   - **Customer Lifetime Value (CLV)**: The total revenue a business can expect from a customer throughout their relationship with the company.
2. **Use Feedback to Improve**:

- Gathering feedback from customers can help you improve their experience and increase the chances they'll come back. Ask for feedback through surveys, reviews, or direct communication.

Encouraging repeat business is crucial for long-term success. By creating loyalty programs, offering personalized experiences, providing excellent customer service, and maintaining consistency, businesses can foster customer loyalty and increase their profitability. Keeping customers coming back is not only about making sales; it's about building strong, lasting relationships that benefit both the business and the customer.

Chapter 46: Building Customer Loyalty Through Email and Social Media

In today's digital age, customer loyalty is more important than ever. With countless options available online, businesses must actively work to retain their customers by building lasting relationships. In this chapter, we will explore how businesses can foster customer loyalty using two key digital tools: email marketing and social media.

Why Customer Loyalty Matters

Customer loyalty refers to the likelihood of customers repeatedly choosing your product or service over a competitor's. Loyal customers are not only more likely to make repeat purchases, but they're also more likely to recommend your brand to others, leave positive reviews, and engage with your content online.

- **Example**: Think about your favorite restaurant. If they consistently provide you with great food and service, you're likely to go back often and even tell your friends about it.

Using Email Marketing to Build Loyalty

1. **Personalized Content**
    - One of the most effective ways to build customer loyalty through email is by personalizing your messages. This means sending emails that are tailored to each customer's preferences, past purchases, or browsing history.
    - **Example**: An online clothing store might send personalized emails suggesting items based on a customer's previous purchases, like recommending winter coats when the cold season starts.
2. **Tips for Personalization:**
    - Use the customer's name in the subject line and body of the email.
    - Send product recommendations based on their interests or past purchases.
    - Create special offers or discounts for birthdays or loyalty milestones.
3. **Regular Engagement**

- Keeping your customers engaged with your brand through regular communication is key. Send newsletters that include updates about new products, exclusive offers, and company news to keep them interested.
- **Example**: A bakery could send out monthly newsletters featuring new seasonal items, upcoming events, and behind-the-scenes stories.

4. **Exclusive Offers for Subscribers**
   - Reward your email subscribers by offering them exclusive deals or early access to new products. This makes them feel like valued members of your community, increasing their loyalty.
   - **Example**: A skincare brand might offer email subscribers a 15% discount on their next purchase or early access to a limited-edition product.
5. **Customer Feedback and Surveys**
   - Asking for customer feedback through emails can make customers feel that their opinions are valued. It also gives businesses valuable insights into how to improve products and services.
   - **Example**: After a purchase, an online bookstore might send a survey asking customers to rate their experience and suggest improvements.

Using Social Media to Build Loyalty

1. **Engaging Content**
   - Social media is a great tool for engaging with your customers in a more casual and interactive way. Posting fun, relevant content that your customers can relate to helps strengthen the connection between them and your brand.
   - **Example**: A coffee shop might post behind-the-scenes videos of how their drinks are made or run a poll asking customers what flavor of the month they'd like to see next.
2. **Building a Community**
   - Social media allows businesses to build a sense of community around their brand. This can be achieved by responding to comments, interacting with followers, and creating content that encourages conversations.

- **Example**: A fitness brand might create a Facebook group where members can share workout tips, progress photos, and success stories, fostering a supportive community.

3. **Running Contests and Giveaways**
   - Hosting contests and giveaways on social media is a fun way to keep your audience engaged and attract new followers. People love the chance to win something, and this can create excitement around your brand.
   - **Example**: A beauty brand could run a contest asking followers to share their favorite makeup look using the brand's products, with the chance to win a free product bundle.
4. **Showcasing User-Generated Content**
   - One way to make customers feel special is by showcasing content they've created. This could include photos or testimonials of them using your product, which also serves as free promotion for your brand.
   - **Example**: A home décor store might repost photos from customers who have shared images of their decorated homes using the store's products, giving the customers a shout-out while showcasing the brand.

Combining Email and Social Media for Maximum Impact

1. **Cross-Promote Your Channels**
   - Encourage your email subscribers to follow you on social media and vice versa. By doing this, you're ensuring that customers can stay connected with your brand across different platforms.
   - **Example**: A clothing brand might include social media links at the bottom of its emails, inviting customers to follow them for exclusive behind-the-scenes content.
2. **Create Consistent Messaging**
   - Make sure that your messaging is consistent across both email and social media. If you're running a special promotion, announce it both in emails and on social platforms to maximize its reach.
   - **Example**: A tech company launching a new product could send a promotional email while also sharing sneak peeks and countdowns on social media.

3. **Exclusive Offers Across Platforms**
    - Use each platform to offer different perks. For example, you can offer email subscribers exclusive discounts and social media followers access to special contests or behind-the-scenes content.
    - **Example**: A fitness apparel brand could offer an email-exclusive discount code, while running a giveaway for social media followers.

Building customer loyalty through email and social media is all about creating meaningful and personalized connections. By consistently engaging with customers, offering exclusive content, and making them feel valued, businesses can foster lasting relationships. The combination of thoughtful email marketing and interactive social media presence ensures that your customers will keep coming back.

Part 14: Sales and Distribution Channels

Chapter 47: Direct-to-Consumer Sales Strategies

Direct-to-Consumer (DTC) sales are becoming increasingly popular for businesses that want to sell their products directly to customers without using third-party retailers or middlemen. In this chapter, we'll explore what DTC sales are, why they are important, and how businesses can use them to build stronger relationships with their customers and increase profits.

What Are Direct-to-Consumer (DTC) Sales?

Direct-to-consumer sales refer to selling products or services directly to customers through your own website, store, or platform without relying on retailers or other distributors. This allows businesses to have full control over their branding, pricing, and customer experience.

- **Example**: A clothing brand might sell its products exclusively through its online store rather than offering them at department stores.

Why Are Direct-to-Consumer Sales Important?

1. **Control Over Customer Experience**
    - When you sell directly to customers, you have full control over how they experience your brand. This means you can create a personalized shopping experience, offer exceptional customer service, and ensure that your branding is consistent across all channels.
    - **Example**: A business selling skincare products online can include personalized thank-you notes or offer free samples with each order, which adds a special touch to the customer experience.
2. **Higher Profit Margins**

- By eliminating middlemen, businesses can keep more of their profits. Since there are no retailers or distributors taking a cut of the sales, businesses can sell their products at competitive prices while still making a profit.
- **Example**: A jewelry brand selling directly to customers via their website can offer lower prices compared to those found in retail stores, as they don't have to account for retailer markups.

3. **Direct Customer Relationships**
    - DTC sales allow businesses to build direct relationships with their customers. By interacting with customers directly, businesses can collect valuable feedback, understand their preferences, and tailor future products to meet their needs.
    - **Example**: A small business might collect email addresses through its online store and send personalized marketing emails based on customers' previous purchases.
4. **Data Collection**
    - When businesses sell directly, they can gather customer data that can help improve marketing strategies. This data includes customer demographics, purchasing behaviors, and website activity.
    - **Example**: A business might notice that customers frequently abandon their carts at the checkout stage. Using this information, the company could send follow-up emails or offer a discount to encourage customers to complete their purchases.

Effective DTC Sales Strategies

1. **Build a User-Friendly Website**
    - Your website is your primary sales channel in a DTC model, so it needs to be easy to navigate, mobile-friendly, and fast-loading. Make sure your website clearly showcases your products, includes detailed descriptions, and makes it simple for customers to make a purchase.
    - **Example**: An online bookstore could have a well-organized website with sections for different genres, customer reviews, and easy checkout options to enhance the user experience.
2. **Leverage Social Media**

- Social media platforms like Instagram, Facebook, and TikTok are powerful tools for promoting your products and driving traffic to your website. Use engaging content, such as product demonstrations, customer testimonials, and behind-the-scenes videos, to connect with your audience and encourage them to visit your site.
- **Example**: A beauty brand could create makeup tutorials using its products and share them on Instagram, directing viewers to their online store to purchase the featured items.

3. **Offer Excellent Customer Service**
    - Since customers interact directly with your business in a DTC model, customer service is critical. Offer quick and helpful support through live chat, email, or phone, and make the returns and exchange process simple.
    - **Example**: An electronics store could offer 24/7 customer service chat support to assist customers with troubleshooting or product questions, ensuring a smooth shopping experience.
4. **Use Email Marketing**
    - Email marketing is a highly effective way to build relationships with your customers. Use email to send personalized product recommendations, exclusive offers, and updates on new product launches.
    - **Example**: A clothing brand could send personalized emails to customers based on their past purchases, such as recommending new arrivals in a customer's preferred style.
5. **Create Subscription Services**
    - Subscription services are an excellent way to ensure repeat business. By offering subscription plans for regular delivery of products, such as monthly skincare or coffee boxes, businesses can guarantee a steady stream of revenue.
    - **Example**: A coffee company could offer a subscription service where customers receive freshly roasted coffee beans every month, tailored to their taste preferences.

Challenges of Direct-to-Consumer Sales

1. **Increased Responsibility**

- Without retailers, businesses are fully responsible for everything, from order fulfillment to customer service. This means they need to invest in efficient logistics, customer support, and marketing strategies.
- **Example**: A company that sells handmade furniture directly to customers must ensure they have a reliable system for shipping large items and handling potential customer complaints or returns.

2. **Marketing Costs**
    - Since DTC businesses don't rely on retailers to promote their products, they must invest more heavily in marketing. This includes digital marketing, social media ads, influencer partnerships, and more.
    - **Example**: A cosmetics company selling exclusively online might spend a significant amount on Facebook ads to attract new customers and drive sales.

Direct-to-consumer sales strategies give businesses more control over their products, pricing, and customer relationships, leading to higher profit margins and greater brand loyalty. However, this model requires a strong online presence, excellent customer service, and a well-thought-out marketing plan. By building a user-friendly website, leveraging social media, and offering personalized customer experiences, businesses can thrive in the DTC space and create long-lasting relationships with their customers.

Chapter 48: Collaborating with Retailers and Distributors

Collaborating with retailers and distributors is one of the most effective ways for a business to expand its reach and grow its customer base. In this chapter, we'll explore the benefits of working with third-party partners and explain how businesses can form successful collaborations to increase sales and improve distribution.

Why Collaborate with Retailers and Distributors?

Collaborating with retailers and distributors can help businesses scale by reaching customers they wouldn't be able to access on their own. Retailers and distributors act as middlemen between businesses and consumers, making products available in a broader range of physical or online stores. This means more exposure for your brand, leading to increased sales and brand awareness. Here's why partnering with retailers and distributors is beneficial:

1. **Wider Market Reach**
    - When your products are placed in retail stores or online marketplaces, you instantly tap into a larger audience that already trusts these platforms. Retailers have a loyal customer base, and having your products available in their stores increases your visibility.
    - **Example**: A small local candle-making business partners with a large retailer like Walmart. This allows the candle company to reach thousands of customers across the country without having to open its own stores.
2. **Distribution Expertise**
    - Distributors specialize in getting products from manufacturers to retailers and customers. They have the expertise, networks, and infrastructure to handle logistics, allowing businesses to focus on what they do best—creating products.
    - **Example**: A beverage company might collaborate with a distributor who handles warehousing, transportation, and delivery, ensuring the drinks are stocked in supermarkets and convenience stores efficiently.
3. **Lower Costs**

- By partnering with retailers and distributors, businesses can reduce the cost of handling logistics themselves. It can be expensive for small or growing businesses to build their own distribution systems, so outsourcing this function can save time and money.
- **Example**: A small clothing brand may not have the resources to ship individual orders, but by working with a distributor, they can ensure their products reach different stores without bearing the full cost of shipping.

How to Collaborate with Retailers and Distributors

1. **Identify Potential Partners**
   - The first step in collaborating with retailers and distributors is identifying the right partners for your brand. Look for companies that align with your business values, have access to your target audience, and can help you achieve your goals.
   - **Example**: A luxury skincare brand might target high-end department stores like Nordstrom or Sephora rather than budget retailers, as these partners cater to the right customer demographic.
2. **Negotiate Terms and Conditions**
   - When collaborating with a retailer or distributor, it's important to establish clear terms. This includes negotiating how much inventory they will carry, the pricing structure, and who is responsible for shipping and returns. These agreements should be in writing to avoid misunderstandings.
   - **Example**: A tech company might negotiate that a retailer must carry a certain number of units in stock at all times and that the retailer is responsible for return policies.
3. **Ensure Consistent Branding**
   - When your products are being sold through third-party retailers or distributors, it's essential to ensure that your branding remains consistent across all platforms. Make sure that your logo, packaging, and marketing materials are consistent, so customers recognize your product no matter where they buy it.
   - **Example**: A coffee brand might create strict guidelines for how their logo is displayed on partner websites and in physical stores to maintain brand integrity.
4. **Provide Retailer Support**

- To make the partnership a success, businesses should provide their retail and distribution partners with the necessary support. This could include providing marketing materials, training their sales team, or offering promotions to drive sales.
- **Example**: A home appliance manufacturer might provide in-store product demonstrations or online tutorials for retail partners to help explain the features of their products to customers.

Overcoming Challenges in Retail and Distribution Partnerships

While collaborating with retailers and distributors has many benefits, it also comes with challenges. Some of these challenges include:

1. **Loss of Control**
    - When you sell through retailers, you lose some control over how your product is marketed and presented. This can lead to inconsistencies in how your brand is perceived by customers.
    - **Solution**: Ensure that you provide retailers with detailed branding guidelines and check in regularly to monitor how your products are displayed.
2. **Lower Profit Margins**
    - When working with retailers, businesses usually sell products to them at wholesale prices, which are lower than the retail price. This can lead to smaller profit margins compared to selling directly to customers.
    - **Solution**: Balance your direct-to-consumer sales with retail partnerships. Selling on your own website at full price allows you to maintain higher margins while still benefiting from the wider reach of retailers.
3. **Inventory Management**
    - Retailers and distributors will expect businesses to provide a steady supply of products, which can be difficult if your business is growing quickly or experiencing supply chain challenges.
    - **Solution**: Work closely with your distributor to manage inventory levels and communicate any delays in advance to avoid stock shortages.

Expanding Your Reach through Online Retailers

In addition to physical stores, businesses can collaborate with online retailers to expand their reach. E-commerce platforms like Amazon, Etsy, and Walmart Marketplace allow businesses to reach a global audience without the need for brick-and-mortar locations.

1. **Benefits of Online Retail Partnerships**
   - Online platforms provide access to millions of customers around the world. They also offer a convenient shopping experience for customers who prefer to shop from home.
   - **Example**: A handmade jewelry brand might sell its products on Etsy, reaching customers worldwide without needing a physical storefront.
2. **Managing Online Partnerships**
   - Selling through online retailers requires careful management of your online storefront, including keeping product listings updated, responding to customer inquiries, and managing reviews. Ensure that your product descriptions are clear and that customers can easily find the information they need.
   - **Example**: A company selling kitchen gadgets on Amazon should regularly update product listings with high-quality images and accurate descriptions to attract more customers and minimize returns.

Collaborating with retailers and distributors is a powerful way for businesses to expand their reach, increase sales, and grow their brand presence. By carefully selecting the right partners, negotiating favorable terms, and maintaining strong relationships, businesses can successfully navigate the world of retail and distribution partnerships. Remember, while working with third-party partners can be complex, the rewards are well worth the effort as they allow businesses to scale faster and reach a wider audience.

Chapter 49: Setting Competitive Pricing for Products and Services

Pricing is one of the most critical aspects of running a successful business. It directly impacts your revenue, profitability, and how customers perceive your brand. In this chapter, we'll break down how to develop a competitive pricing strategy that balances customer demand, market trends, and profitability.

Why Pricing is Important

Setting the right price for your products or services is key to driving sales and ensuring your business remains profitable. If your prices are too high, you might lose customers to competitors. If your prices are too low, you could struggle to cover costs and make a profit. Therefore, a thoughtful pricing strategy is essential to maintaining a successful business.

1. **Customer Perception**: Pricing influences how customers perceive your brand. Higher prices might signal premium quality, while lower prices might suggest affordability or lower quality.
   - **Example**: A high-end electronics company may set higher prices to communicate superior technology and performance.
2. **Profitability**: Your pricing needs to cover costs like production, marketing, and distribution while leaving enough profit for your business to grow.
   - **Example**: A clothing brand that sells t-shirts must factor in the cost of materials, production, and shipping when determining its price.
3. **Market Positioning**: How you position your products in the market can also impact your pricing strategy. Are you aiming to be a premium brand, or do you want to attract customers with affordable prices?
   - **Example**: A coffee shop might offer both luxury and budget-friendly drinks to appeal to different customer segments.

Steps to Develop a Competitive Pricing Strategy

1. **Understand Your Costs**
   - The first step in setting a price is understanding all the costs involved in producing and delivering your product or service. This includes materials, labor, shipping, and marketing costs.

- **Tip**: Make sure your prices cover all your costs and still leave room for profit.

2. **Research Competitors**
   - Look at what your competitors are charging for similar products or services. This will give you a sense of where your pricing fits into the market.
   - **Example**: If you own a bakery and your competitors sell cupcakes for $3 each, pricing yours between $3 and $4 might be appropriate, depending on factors like quality and location.
3. **Know Your Target Audience**
   - Your pricing should reflect the expectations and preferences of your target audience. For example, luxury shoppers may expect higher prices, while bargain hunters will be more price-sensitive.
   - **Example**: A technology company selling to business professionals might price its software higher than a competitor targeting students.
4. **Choose a Pricing Model**
   - There are several pricing models you can choose from, depending on your goals and industry:
     - **Cost-Plus Pricing**: Add a fixed percentage to your costs to determine the selling price. This is a straightforward approach that ensures you make a profit on each sale.
       - **Example**: If a company spends $10 to make a product and adds a 50% markup, the selling price would be $15.
     - **Value-Based Pricing**: Price based on the value your product offers to customers rather than the cost to make it.
       - **Example**: A company selling software that saves customers time might charge more because of the high value it provides, even if it's inexpensive to produce.
     - **Penetration Pricing**: Set a low price to enter a competitive market and attract customers, then gradually increase the price.
       - **Example**: A new streaming service might offer a lower subscription fee to gain users, then raise prices once they've built a loyal customer base.
5. **Factor in Psychological Pricing**

- Psychological pricing involves strategies that make customers perceive the price as more attractive.
  - **Odd Pricing**: Setting prices just below a round number, like $9.99 instead of $10, can make products seem cheaper.
  - **Bundle Pricing**: Offering a group of products or services at a discounted rate can make the overall offer more appealing.
    - **Example**: A cosmetics company could offer a skincare bundle at $50 instead of selling individual products for a total of $60.

Adjusting Prices Based on Market Trends

Pricing isn't something you set once and forget. You need to regularly adjust your prices based on changes in the market, customer demand, and costs.

1. **Market Demand**: If demand for your product increases, you may be able to raise your prices. Conversely, if demand drops, you might need to lower prices to stay competitive.
   - **Example**: During a holiday season, a toy company might increase prices due to high demand for a popular product.
2. **Competition**: If competitors lower their prices, you may need to adjust yours to remain competitive, especially if customers are highly price-sensitive.
   - **Example**: A fitness app may offer discounts or promotions to compete with similar apps in a crowded marketplace.
3. **Costs**: If your costs increase (e.g., due to higher shipping fees or material costs), you may need to raise prices to maintain profitability.
   - **Example**: A restaurant may increase menu prices if the cost of ingredients rises significantly.

When to Use Discounts and Promotions

Discounts and promotions can be effective tools for driving short-term sales, but you need to use them carefully to avoid damaging your brand's value.

1. **Attract New Customers**: Offering a discount to first-time buyers can encourage them to try your product.
   - **Example**: A subscription box service might offer 20% off the first month for new subscribers.

2. **Clear Out Old Inventory**: If you have products that aren't selling well, running a sale can help clear out old stock.
    - **Example**: A clothing store might hold an end-of-season sale to make room for new inventory.
3. **Drive Holiday or Event-Based Sales**: Offering special promotions around holidays or events can create urgency and boost sales.
    - **Example**: Many online retailers offer Black Friday deals to attract holiday shoppers.

Setting competitive prices is essential for balancing profitability with customer demand. By understanding your costs, researching competitors, and choosing the right pricing model, you can develop a strategy that works for your business. Regularly reviewing your prices and adjusting them based on market conditions will help ensure that your pricing stays competitive and aligned with your business goals.

Part 15: Future Growth and Business Operations

Chapter 50: Planning for Business Scalability

Scalability is essential for businesses looking to grow without compromising quality or customer satisfaction. In this final chapter, we will explore strategies that help businesses scale operations efficiently, ensuring they can handle increased demand while continuing to meet customer expectations. The goal is to build a framework that supports long-term growth and profitability.

What is Scalability?

Scalability refers to a business's ability to grow and expand its operations without a significant increase in costs. A scalable business can handle a growing workload or customer base without sacrificing efficiency or performance.

- **Example**: An e-commerce store expanding from selling 100 products a day to 1,000 without needing to increase staff by the same ratio. By automating order fulfillment and customer service, the business can grow without dramatically increasing its expenses.

Steps to Plan for Scalability

1. **Streamline Operations**
    - Before scaling, businesses must ensure their current processes are as efficient as possible. Streamlining operations involves eliminating unnecessary steps and automating tasks to save time and resources.
    - **Example**: A bakery might automate inventory management, ensuring ingredients are always stocked and reducing time spent manually tracking supplies.
2. **Invest in Technology**

- Technology plays a critical role in scalability. Businesses can leverage software to automate tasks, track customer data, and manage operations. Cloud-based systems allow for flexibility, ensuring that companies can scale up without massive infrastructure costs.
- **Example**: A small clothing brand could use cloud-based inventory management and sales tracking software to monitor stock levels and sales trends across multiple locations without the need for on-site servers.

3. **Build a Strong Team**
   - Scaling often requires growing your team. However, it's not just about hiring more people—it's about hiring the right people. A strong team with clear roles and responsibilities will help maintain quality as your business grows.
   - **Example**: A tech startup might hire additional developers and a dedicated customer service team to handle increasing demand, allowing the founders to focus on strategy and innovation.
4. **Focus on Customer Experience**
   - As businesses grow, it's important not to lose sight of the customer experience. Ensure that customer service, product quality, and delivery times remain consistent, even as your company expands.
   - **Example**: An online retailer scaling up could implement an automated chatbot for basic customer service inquiries while maintaining a dedicated support team for complex issues.
5. **Diversify Revenue Streams**
   - One way to scale effectively is by diversifying your revenue streams. Offering new products, services, or pricing models can help grow your business without relying too heavily on one source of income.
   - **Example**: A gym might offer personal training sessions, online fitness classes, and a line of branded workout gear to generate multiple income streams.

Key Areas to Focus On for Scalability

1. **Operations Management**

   - Streamlining your business operations ensures that everything runs smoothly as demand increases. This includes optimizing workflows, automating repetitive tasks, and ensuring that your supply chain can handle more orders.
   - **Tip**: Use project management software to keep track of tasks and deadlines as your team grows.
2. **Financial Planning**
   - Expanding a business often requires investment. Make sure you have a solid financial plan that includes budgeting for growth, securing funding if needed, and tracking cash flow.
   - **Example**: A startup might secure venture capital funding to scale quickly, but they must have a clear plan for how that money will be spent to drive growth.
3. **Marketing Strategy**
   - To scale, you'll need to attract more customers. Expanding your marketing efforts, whether through social media, paid advertising, or content marketing, will help reach new audiences and generate demand.
   - **Example**: A small coffee shop looking to expand might launch an online store, selling branded merchandise and coffee beans nationwide while increasing its social media presence to drive traffic to the site.
4. **Supply Chain and Distribution**
   - As demand increases, so will the need for efficient supply chain and distribution channels. Ensure your suppliers can keep up with increased production, and explore partnerships with third-party logistics providers to handle shipping.
   - **Example**: A skincare brand scaling up might partner with a fulfillment center that manages inventory and shipping, ensuring fast and reliable delivery to customers.
5. **Product and Service Development**
   - Scaling isn't just about doing more of the same; it often involves developing new products or services to meet customer needs. Keep innovating and improving your offerings to stay competitive.
   - **Example**: A software company scaling up might release new features and integrations to attract larger clients and expand its market.

Challenges of Scaling a Business

1. **Maintaining Quality**
   - One of the biggest challenges of scaling is maintaining the same level of quality that initially attracted customers. As demand increases, there may be pressure to cut corners, but this can harm your brand in the long run.
   - **Solution**: Implement quality control processes and regularly review customer feedback to ensure that your products or services meet expectations.
2. **Managing Cash Flow**
   - Scaling often requires significant upfront investment, whether it's in inventory, staff, or technology. Without careful financial planning, you may struggle to manage cash flow as you grow.
   - **Solution**: Maintain a strong financial cushion and regularly update your budget to reflect changes in revenue and expenses.
3. **Scaling Too Quickly**
   - Growing too quickly can overwhelm your team, your supply chain, and your finances. It's important to scale at a pace that your business can handle without sacrificing quality or profitability.
   - **Solution**: Set realistic growth targets and regularly review your progress to ensure you're scaling sustainably.

Planning for business scalability involves more than just growing in size—it's about creating a sustainable framework that allows your company to handle increased demand without compromising quality or efficiency. By streamlining operations, investing in technology, and maintaining a strong focus on customer experience, businesses can scale successfully and thrive in the long term. Keep your goals clear, ensure your team is prepared, and always be ready to adapt as your business grows.

NOW ON AMAZON

By Author C. G. Mitchell

Other Books Available

InclusiveMediaInk.com
Other books by C. G. Mitchell under the pen name
Cheri Lawrence

Children's Books Available On Amazon

Coloring Books Available
On Amazon

Other Books Available at
InclusiveMediaInk.com

HOME DÉCOR

Available at InclusiveMediaInk.com

Designs by my husband Jerome Lawrence

Curtains, Bedspreads, Sheets, Pillows, Table Cloths, Table Runners, Napkins and Wallpaper

Clothing Available at InclusiveMediaInk.com

Tote Bags Available at InclusiveMediaInk.com

Weekend Bags Available at InclusiveMediaInk.com

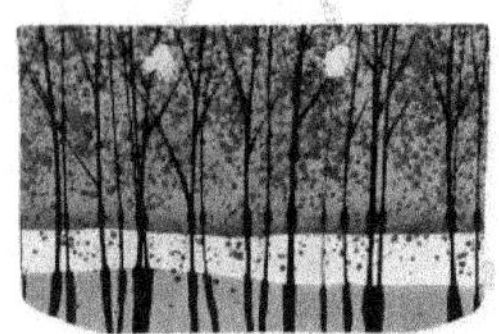

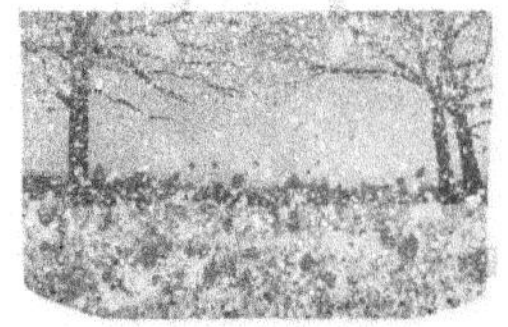

Framed Art Prints Available from InclusiveMediaInk.com

www.ingramcontent.com/pod-product-compliance
Lightning Source LLC
Chambersburg PA
CBHW052312220526
45472CB00001B/77

9798344676111